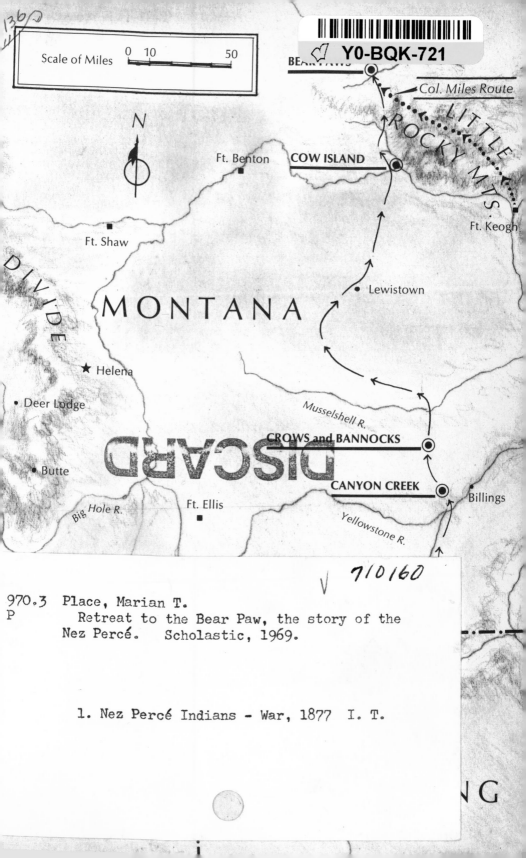

Scale of Miles
0   10   50

BEAR PAWS

Col. Miles Route

LITTLE ROCKY MTS.

Ft. Benton   COW ISLAND

N

Ft. Keogh

Ft. Shaw

MONTANA

Lewistown

★ Helena

• Deer Lodge

Musselshell R.

DISCARD

CROWS and BANNOCKS

• Butte

CANYON CREEK   Billings

Big Hole R.   Ft. Ellis

Yellowstone R.

N G

i

MARION T. PLACE

RETREAT
to the
BEAR PAW

THE STORY OF THE NEZ PERCÉ

FOUR WINDS PRESS / NEW YORK

To Meda Johnson

Published by Four Winds Press
A Division of Scholastic Magazines, Inc., New York, N.Y.
Copyright © 1969 by Marion T. Place
All rights reserved.
Printed in the United States of America

Library of Congress Catalogue Card Number 71-81700

CONTENTS

I   A Vengeance Raid

The young Nez Percé warriors were angry. For hours they had sat about the council fire, in the second rank, listening to the chiefs and old men mourn the evil times that had befallen their people. Again and again Wahlitits and his hot-headed friends leaped to their feet and argued for war against the whites who had robbed and killed their relatives. They said if the old men would not put on their war paint and avenge these wrongs, the young men would strike on their own.

But their taunts were in vain. The leaders, seated in the first rank, stubbornly rejected the idea of a vengeance raid. Looking Glass, chief of the Clearwater River band, warned the youths to leave the arrows in their quivers, lest they bring down war upon the people. He reminded them that once the Nez Percés had been strong, rich in horses, cattle and robes, and free to roam their far-flung mountain home. But now they were divided, band against band, cousin against cousin, and forced to settle on a cramped reservation. There was no other choice if they wished to survive as a people, if the women and children were not to suffer.

One after another the young men declared they would rather die in battle than give up their freedom without a fight. They beat their breasts with clenched fists and vowed they would not walk with bowed heads through the reservation gate and be counted in the same way white men numbered their livestock. They were not cattle. They were men!

Wahlitits shouted that for two years the head men had persuaded him not to seek revenge for the cold-blooded murder of his father. But he could wait no longer! He wanted war!

Tough old White Bird, chief of the Salmon River band, waved his eagle-feather fan to signify he wished to speak. He soothed Wahlitits' vanity by saying what a good shooter and fighter he was when the Nez Percés fought their long-time enemies, the Bannocks. He said every one knew Wahlitits was brave. Wahlitits did not have to cry for war to prove he was a man. Of course, the seventy-year-old leader added, he could not tell Wahlitits what to do. It was the Nez Percé way to allow a man complete freedom of action, to do as he pleased, even after his chief and family had persuaded him not to seek revenge. But the young man must consider this—if he struck out against his father's murderer, then General Howard would send the soldiers against his people.

The remaining chiefs, subchiefs, and medicine men spoke in turn, saying they did not want war. They would do as their fathers had done, and their grandfathers, who had promised the two white captains Lewis and Clark that they would live in peace forever with their white brothers. That promise was the reason they had agreed to leave their long-time campsites in the mountain valleys and deep canyons of Oregon and Idaho and move peacefully onto the reservation.

Finally, Looking Glass placed his thumb over the coals in the stone ceremonial pipe to show that they were cool and the talking must end. Since he was the greatest buffalo hunter and fighter among them, he was listened to with respect by the elders and young alike. He reminded those present unnecessarily, for he was a windy talker, that almost thirty days ago the chiefs had promised General Howard their people would report to the reservation not later than June 14, 1877. So they had struck their lodges and rounded up their horses and cattle and gathered for the last time at Tepahlewam for their traditional summer rendezvous. Now it was June 12. For two more days the people would visit and sing and dance in the old way. Then they would move a few miles to the southernmost boundary of the reservation and press on sixty miles to the headquarters. After General Howard and the agent in charge there had greeted them and distributed presents, they would move, band by band, to the separate tracts which the chiefs had chosen for them.

There will be no war, Looking Glass stated emphatically as he turned the pipe over and tapped the cold ashes onto the ground. That ended the council.

The chiefs filed out into the brilliant sunshine. To all

outward appearances the warm June day differed little from others spent at Tepahlewam, a beautiful meadow five miles west of present-day Grangeville, Idaho. Practically all of the more than sixty lodges raised this year belonged to four Nez Percé bands. One was the Salmon River band which came from the rugged gold-bearing canyon country south of Tepahlewam. The head man was seventy-year-old Peopeo Kiskiak Hihih. Although this translates to White Goose, he was widely known as White Bird. In his youth, he had been a great hunter and warrior and was still a vigorous leader.

The second band came from the upper reaches of the Snake River. The chief was Toolhoolhoolzote, a name difficult to translate. Over seventy, he was a homely, wrathful fellow whom government officials called "the cross-grained growler." The third was the Clearwater River band headed by the tall, strong forty-five-year-old Looking Glass. This band's village was some twenty miles away along a small tributary of the Clearwater River, and actually lay within the limits of the reservation. But because Looking Glass had refused to sign a treaty in 1863, General Howard considered them hostile to the Government. He insisted they never set foot off the reservation, give up their fall hunts, and be "good Indians."

The fourth and largest band at Tepahlewam came from the remote, mountain-ringed, three-thousand-foot-high Wallowa *(wah-láh-wah)* Valley of northeastern Oregon. The chief of the Wallowas was a handsome, intelligent man whose Indian name was Hin-mah-too-yah-let-keht, or Thunder Traveling to Loftier Mountain Heights. White men called him Joseph. The youngest of the four chiefs, thirty-seven-year-old Joseph was not a buffalo hunter, nor

Chief Joseph, as he looked in 1896.

experienced in tribal warfare. His younger brother, Ollokot, to whom he was devoted, was the chief warrior of the Wallowas. Neither Joseph nor Ollokot could attend the council because they were butchering cattle at the herd ground several miles away.

For centuries the Nez Percés, who numbered between four and six thousand persons, traveled from their small independent and isolated villages to Tepahlewam for an annual reunion. Usually the rendezvous was a happy occasion marked with feasts, dances, games, and much gossip. But this year sorrow underlay the festivities. No more than six hundred were present, because the Nez Percés were divided into two factions. One included those bands who had signed a treaty with the government in 1863 whereby they agreed to confine themselves to a reservation in northern Idaho. The government called them Treaty Indians. Since the soldiers who kept them under surveillance would not permit them to leave the reservation, the Treaty bands could not attend the reunion. They were subdued now, having given up the old-time carefree nomadic life to become farmers, or subsist on government handouts.

The other faction was made up mostly of four bands camped at Tepahlewam. They had refused to sign the treaty, and none except Looking Glass lived on the reservation. They were all called non-Treaty Indians. They had withdrawn in anger from the council of 1863 and retired to their villages, hoping to keep away from white people. But this was impossible. After prospectors discovered gold in the Nez Percé country, thousands rushed into the Idaho territory. The non-Treaty bands were overrun by white men who mistreated and robbed and even killed them. Conditions worsened year after year until finally, in May of 1877, General Oliver O. Howard called the non-Treaty chiefs and leaders to a council at Fort Lapwai. He said that for their own protection, the bands must move onto the reservation. They must report to the agent in charge not later than June 14. Then he added, "If you let the time run over one day, the soldiers will be there to drive you onto the reservation, and all your cattle and horses outside of the reservation at that time will fall into the hands of the white men."

The chiefs heard the threat in those words and agreed to meet the deadline. They also promised to come in peacefully. This is why, when they met again at Tepahlewam, they would not allow Wahlitits and the other young hotheads to harangue them into starting a war. Now the council was over, the talking finished. They would return to their lodges and rest before the evening's festivities. Meanwhile the women and girls who had been digging camas bulbs all day spread them out to dry on skins laid alongside the tepees. The children still romped about, while the old people, many partially or wholly blind, were content to warm themselves in the sunshine.

The scene was a peaceful one, like old times, except in the cottonwood grove where Wahlitits and the young men had withdrawn. They milled about, daring one another to lead a raid against the Indian-haters who had established small ranches near Tepahlewam. Each warrior boasted of his bravery and prowess as a fighter. According to an eyewitness account, one shouted that the chiefs had gone in peace to talk with General Howard at Fort Lapwai, and he had threatened to turn the soldiers against them if they did not report to the reservation agency by

*A Nez Percé brave with a white
heron's wing fan. From a
photograph taken in 1905.*

June 14. "General Howard has shown us the rifle," he raged. "We answer, 'Yes.' We will stir up a fight for him. We will start his war!"

We know what he said because many years later he and others told their stories to a friendly white rancher named L. V. McWhorter, who wrote down the words just as the Indians spoke them. The dialogue throughout this book is drawn from those stories.

Next, the young warriors saddled their war ponies and prepared for a raid. They stripped down to breechcloths and moccasins, mixed war paint with grease and applied it with great care. They lined the center part of their hair with red, daubed their foreheads with red and orange, and dotted their eyelids, cheeks, and bodies with green, yellow, and black specks. Each line and dot had a meaning. A few donned feathered headdresses.

Others wore head covers which represented animals sacred to them—wolf, grizzly, buffalo, and elk. They adorned their bodies and braids with ermine tails, bear-claw necklaces, and eagle feathers. Some armed themselves with bows and quivers of arrows, the tips dipped in rattlesnake venom, while others brandished war clubs, lances, and old cap-and-ball revolvers.

As each one mounted, he rode to the grove and shouted until all were present. An argument broke out over who should lead the raid. After it was settled, they decided to ride around the campsite, past every lodge, so the people could see how brave they were and hear them boast of their plans. They slammed their heels into their ponies' flanks and paraded about, brandishing their weapons, whooping, and riding back and forth in simulated war maneuvers. The column of horsemen was brought up in the rear by two warriors mounted on the same steed. This was the place of honor, because in actual warfare only the bravest rode in such an exposed and dangerous position. There had been no quarrel about who should have this favored post. Those named were two of White Bird's warriors, Wahlitits (Shore Crossing) and his cousin Sarpsis Ilppilp (Red Moccasin Tops). More than any young man present, Wahlitits was the most excited and spoiling for trouble.

Since the campsite extended over several acres, more than an hour passed in the demonstration. At first the people watched it, and a few shouted encouragement. But then they turned to hauling wood and water, or eating, or dressing for the evening's program of singing and dancing. The young men saw the plumes of smoke rising from the campfires and smelled the good aroma of roasting meat. They heard the musicians testing their drums and saw the pretty girls decking themselves with beads and paint. Then the leader remembered that the warriors had not prayed for victory, nor purified themselves, as they must if they wished to escape unharmed from a battle. He shouted all this to his companions. One after another decided to forget about war until some other time. They dispersed to their lodges.

Unfortunately, Wahlitits thoughtlessly rode his pony across the camas bulbs which the wife of Yellow Grizzly Bear had spread to dry. The husband was furious and taunted, "You, Wahlitits! You ride around, shouting how brave you are. You ruin my woman's food. If you are brave, why don't you kill the white man who murdered your father?"

Stung by this insult, Wahlitits exclaimed, "You will be

sorry for your words!" He rode to his family's lodge and told his cousin to turn the pony onto the grazing ground. Then he entered the lodge and flung himself down on his bed. He would not speak, nor could he be enticed to attend the dance. Since it was the Nez Percé way to let a person do as he pleased, the family left him alone. So for many hours he brooded over Yellow Grizzly Bear's insult to his honor. No longer could he be denied revenge!

Very early the next morning he roused Sarpsis Ilppilp and a teenaged nephew named Swan Necklace. They roped their ponies and rode to the ranch of the man who had killed Wahlitits' father in a quarrel over use of his land. Since Swan Necklace was not yet seventeen, he could not do a man's deeds. He was left to hold the ponies in a thicket of tall chokecherry bushes. Wahlitits and Sarpsis Ilppilp crept up on the man's cabin, but he was nowhere to be found. Frustration heightened Wahlitits' lust for killing, so the three moved on to the ranch of an elderly white settler named Richard Devine. This man was a known Indian-hater who always set his vicious dogs on any Indian who came in sight. But today Devine lay ill in bed and was easily overwhelmed.

One killing was not enough. After taking Devine's guns, ammunition, and food, they remembered another Indian-hater and rode toward John Day Creek. Here they shot Henry Elfers, yet did not harm his Indian wife and children. They took more food and ammunition and stole a prized stallion. Very shortly afterwards, they killed two more ranchers and wounded Samuel Benedict at his crossroads store. The latter was hated because he cheated his Indian customers and unlawfully peddled whiskey to them.

Anxious to boast of his deeds, Wahlitits led the way back to Tepahlewam. Rather than involve their families in their terrible deeds, he and his cousin remained at a distance. Just before sunset Swan Necklace, who had held the horses, mounted the stolen stallion and rode into camp, shouting the news from lodge to lodge. He said the two planned more killings the next day and asked any who wished to join them.

Immediately the camp was in an uproar. Some shouted to rally for war. Others were frightened and made ready to flee because white soldiers were sure to retaliate. White Bird and Toolhoolhoolzote quieted their people and forced them to take no action until Joseph was summoned from the butchering grounds. Looking Glass and his Clearwater band had left the day before to return to their village. They had a large herd and garden to tend to, but expected to join the others in reporting to the agency.

In the morning, Two Moons rode out and told Joseph, "War has broken out. Wahlitits has killed four white men and will kill more today!"

Joseph summoned his brother Ollokot, and all raced to camp. There Joseph rode amongst the people, urging them not to flee. If they would wait until the soldiers came, he said he would explain that the people were not to blame for the killings. That way they would not be punished. But the families were terrified of the soldiers. All except the Wallowa band and seventeen warriors belonging to White Bird's band fled Tepahlewam.

The seventeen warriors joined Wahlitits in a bloody vengeance raid against the settlers. Their band had suffered greatly at the hands of the white gold-seekers who had overrun the Salmon River country. Thus every warrior sought revenge for the abuses committed against his family. Their first target was Benedict's store. They killed the owner and scattered the gold dust which the miners had left with him for safekeeping. They also carried off his stock of whiskey, so for two days their drunken whooping echoed throughout the country. As word of the attacks spread to the neighboring ranches, the terrified white families fled toward Lewiston. Still, fourteen settlers died horribly during the raid.

All this happened while Joseph held his Wallowa band at Tepahlewam. The people protested tearfully that the soldiers would not give him a chance to explain, and they would be killed. After a party of white men fired on their tepees, Joseph made a fateful decision. Although his people were blameless, they must not desert their neighbors and cousins. They must join those who had fled.

At long last they must stand up for their rights, even if it meant striking out against their white brothers. The years of striving to be friendly and cooperative had brought them only misery. They did not want to be fenced in like cattle behind the reservation fence. They did not want to give up their large herds and be farmers. They did not want government "protection" and charity. They wanted to live as Indians, not as white people. To defend this right to live as their forefathers had in the Nez Percé country, they were willing to risk death.

But first they would fight.

II   "Stout likely men,
handsom women and verry dressey"

In Nez Percé country, the rising sun first pours its lemon-yellow light on the jagged peaks of the Bitterroot Mountains in western Montana. But it must reach higher to brighten the deeply entrenched canyons of the Salmon and Snake rivers in Idaho. Soon the coniferous forests of eastern Oregon are glowing in blue-green splendor, and the snow-capped Wallowa Mountains have cast off their cloud cover. Throughout the far-flung wilderness, hawks take wing, elk and deer begin to browse, and water ouzels frolic in the swift icy creeks.

Thirteen thousand years had passed since the forefathers of the Nez Percé Indians first drifted into the region. Over the centuries, they came down in small family groups from Alaska where *their* ancient forefathers had stalked the wooly mammoth and big-tusked mastodon. Long after the beasts became extinct, these first families and their descendants continued southward along the western slope of the Rocky Mountains. Eventually some settled along the Snake, Salmon, and Clearwater rivers and their tributaries.

In time, these early native Americans formed tribes with differing languages or dialects. One of them was the Nez Percés, who have their own more fanciful way of describing their beginnings. According to their legends, long ago their people sprang fully-formed from the heart of a monster who dwelt in the Kamiah Valley along the Clearwater River. They called themselves *Chopunnish,* which meant simply "the people." The tribe was made up of numerous small independent bands, each headed by a chief chosen by its people. All told, there were about seventy bands, some numbering three hundred, others as few as twenty. Although their semi-permanent villages were many miles apart, so that each would have hunting and fishing territory sufficient to its needs, there was much intermarrying. The families were closely knit and affectionate, so in order to keep in touch, all the bands came together for an annual reunion in June, which was bulb-gathering time. Tepahlewam was favored because of the immense camas meadows nearby.

By the dawn of the nineteenth century, the Nez Percés no longer draped fur robes and capes of shredded bark over their bodies. Their clothes were tailored and handsomely decorated with elk teeth, shells, and beads. Many of the men were six feet tall and well-formed, and the women comely. They bathed daily, and the young men gained strength and hardiness by swimming in the cold,

An elderly Nez Percé man photographed in 1868.

swift rivers. Food gathering was a family responsibility in which young and old took part. They fished for salmon with nets and spears and hunted game with powerful bows and arrows. The women and girls harvested wild berries and dug cormlike roots called *kouse,* from which they made mush or cakes, and camas lily bulbs which were eaten cooked or raw. They hoarded these along with dried meat and fish in baskets in order to feed their families during the winter. Ordinarily the Nez Percés ate a light meal on rising and a heavy meal in the evening. As did many other Indians, they offered food to visitors regardless of the time of their arrival.

Some villages were located at the bottom of deep canyons where winter temperatures were warmer. They built two kinds of semi-permanent shelters. Some preferred circular pit houses for which large holes were dug four feet in the ground, and walled and roofed with mats woven of reeds and brush. When several families wished to live together for sociability, they constructed longhouses. Instead of being round, these were long buildings, averaging from fifty to eighty feet, although some extended one hundred and fifty feet in length to accommodate twenty or more families. Each family cooked over a separate fire which burned in a trench down the middle of the dwelling. The smoke escaped through a hole in the roof.

Other bands spent most of the year in villages along creek bottoms where high banks provided some protection from the wind. Their dwellings never were arranged in any set plan, although they were likely to be clustered near the lodges of the chiefs. The latter were larger because public meetings were held in them. A large camp might extend along a stream for several miles. When one campsite became too dirty, the people moved to another and let sun, rain, and floodwaters take care of housekeeping chores. Tepees, or portable lodges, made of tanned hides or woven mats, were used when the villagers traveled to Tepahlewam and elsewhere.

Before the white men came, the Nez Percés roamed northward as far as the Coeur d'Alene lakes in present-day Idaho, westward across the valleys of the Imnaha, Wallowa, and Grande Ronde rivers in Oregon, and southward beyond Hell's Canyon of the Snake River, the deepest canyon in all North America. Occasionally, the Oregon bands journeyed down the banks of the Columbia River to The Dalles for a great trading fair. Here they met families from other tribes who lived in the central valleys or along the coast of Oregon and Washington—Yakimas, Palouse, Umatillas, Chinooks, and Klamaths. Before 1800, they learned from the Chinooks about white Russian and American traders and seal hunters. What they heard was not good. Still they gladly traded with the Chinooks for white men's manufactured articles, such as knives, blue and white beads, bits of brass or copper, needles, and cast-iron kettles. They also copied the fashion of the middle Columbia River tribes and pierced their noses with thin shells. These penetrated the septum, or bony wall separating the nostrils.

At one time or another, some of the bands traveled eastward through a pass in the Rocky Mountains in order to hunt buffalo in present-day Montana. Here they visited with the Flathead and Crow tribes. Sometimes they fought, not always successfully, with the warlike Blackfeet and Cheyennes. But their traditional enemies were the Bannocks of Idaho.

The Nez Percés never did develop a tight tribal organization. Until the government forced the designation of a head chief on them in order to simplify treaty negotiations, they had no one who spoke for all the bands. Each band was autonomous. The chief's word was not law; rather, he ruled by persuasion. The Nez Percés treasured individual freedom of action and expression. If a man did not agree with his chief or village council, he could join another. When he waged war, he fought as he thought best and quit the fight whenever he wanted. Anybody could lead a war or raiding party. Others would join or not, depending on the status of the leader as a warrior, his past successes in such ventures, or the whim of the individual. The leader was in full control of the raid, but if any member disagreed at any time with his plans, he simply returned home.

In a sense, the bands developed what historians call "participatory democracy." Such a policy in one form or another had been practiced by *native* Americans centuries before white Europeans came to our Atlantic shores. But often the Nez Percés practiced freedom of action to such an extreme that no man felt any obligation to work or fight for the common good. Thus he could not see that responsibility was an inseparable companion to freedom.

For example, Chief White Bird had persuaded, not ordered, Wahlitits not to seek revenge for his father's murder because this would put both the family and the band in danger of being punished by the soldiers. But when Wahlitits could hold back no longer, he was free to carry out his vengeance raid. Afterwards he and Sarpsis Ilppilp did not rejoin their people, but camped at a distance. They sent in Swan Necklace to tell of their deeds. Thus, the band would not be blamed for what they had done as individuals. Or so they thought.

The Nez Percé women fared much better than those of neighboring tribes. While they worked hard, they were not abused or treated as slaves. They were allowed to express their opinions to their fathers and husbands, and in marriage were treated as partners. Often they married out of choice and were free to marry into another band. As in other tribes, there were more women than men, so the husbands married two or more wives in order to produce enough children to prevent eventual tribal extinction and, equally important, to share the work of gathering food. By tribal law the women had to get along, and older wives could not mistreat the younger ones. Long before white men visited them, the Nez Percés had recognized the value of happy, affectionate family relationships, and this is why harmony was stressed so strongly. Usually those who dwelt in longhouses were related and lived together peacefully, teaching and counseling each other. Since the men were deeply attached to their families, their actions frequently were governed by what was best for them.

Children were almost never disciplined, yet all grew up with a strong sense of family ties. Grandparents had an important role in teaching the children tribal history and correct behavior. As boys grew older, their fathers or older brothers became more important in their training. The girls were trained by their mothers. The father's role was to instruct his sons in the duties of a hunter and warrior, to instill bravery in him, as well as modesty and the ability to get along with others. He taught him horsemanship and how to care for the herds. Boys in their teens

A Nez Percé couple stand before their tepee. The dog is hitched to a travois.

Skin lodges made up the temporary encampment of a small hunting party on the Yellowstone River in 1871. The woman in the foreground is making pemmican.

were allowed to join war parties, first only to herd the ponies, and after they reached the age of seventeen to participate as full-fledged warriors.

Spiritually the Nez Percés worshiped a Great Spirit and considered the earth, which nourished them, their mother. They looked upon the trees, rocks, rivers, animals, and birds as their brothers. No individual, family, or band owned the land, or any portion of it. The chiefs repeatedly explained this to white officials or settlers who insisted the Indians sell their land. They said "No man owns his mother." This belief led to much bitter misunderstanding and bloodshed later on.

By 1730, the Nez Percés had acquired horses, though it is not known how, or from whom. The animals throve on the lush grasslands. The young men quickly learned to ride for hunting and waging war and to breed the horses for stronger conformation. But they did not especially breed nor favor the spotted horses, which modern devotees of the Appaloosa horse now claim.

William Clark, co-leader of the famed Lewis and Clark Expedition, was the first white man to visit the Nez Percés. On September 20, 1805, he and six hunters came down out of the rugged Bitterroot Mountains to the western edge of the present-day Weippe Prairie in Idaho. Through sign language, the red-haired Clark understood he must first smoke a pipe. The interpreter told him, "No smoke, then must fight." Clark promptly sat down and shared a pipe with his hosts. He noted the bits of shell in their noses and wrote in his journal that these people called themselves *"cho pun nish,"* but he named them "Pierced Nose Indians." He added that they were "Stout likely men, handsom women, and verry dressey," as well as proud, dignified, and industrious. Compared to some he had encountered on the westward trek, these were superior Indians.

After Captain Meriwether Lewis and the remainder of the expedition corps arrived, the Indians entertained them with feasting and dancing. More important, using charcoal to draw on whitened elkskin, the chief provided the leaders of the Discovery Corps with a map which untangled the rivers and canyons to the west. With relief, Lewis saw that his men could put dugouts in the Clearwater River and float all the way to the Pacific Ocean. In appreciation for this assistance, he presented the Indians with two American flags, impressing on them that the flags were symbols of peace. In accepting them, the chief promised that he and his brothers would live forever in peace with their white brothers. Afterward Lewis gave the chief a medallion bearing the likeness of President Thomas Jefferson, some tobacco, and trinkets. Then the explorers left their horses in care of the Nez Percés and continued westward. When they returned in the spring on their way back to St. Louis, the members gained back their fattened mounts and parted on good terms.

A few years later French Canadian trappers visited these Indians. Naturally they used French words *(nez percé)* to describe the people with the pierced noses. American fur traders adopted the foreign phrase, but pronounced it phonetically as *"nezz purse." This latter pronunciation still holds.* The Nez Percés were popular with early explorers, trappers, and traders because they were friendly and helpful. But this was because they saw the white men as visitors, merely passing through their territory, and never expected any to remain.

*A sketch made by an Army
officer of the Nez Percés driving
a herd of their famous horses.*

III   A Divided People

At the time Lewis and Clark visited the Nez Percés, the tribe was one of the richest in the Pacific Northwest. Their wealth was based largely on their vast horse herds, but their economy was also strengthened by their rich store of robes, tepees, saddles, clothing, and food. As they began selling their horses to white men, they acquired in exchange gold coins, a few guns, wool blankets, and copper kettles. But when they observed the white men's greater wealth in guns and manufactured goods, they felt this was the result of the whites having a more powerful medicine, or religion. They reasoned that if they learned from the "black book," or Bible, their wealth would increase and their enemies be vanquished. At no time did the Nez Percés intend to forsake the faith of their forefathers for Christianity. They wanted to learn of it only as an *addition* to their own beliefs.

So, in 1831, seven Nez Percé and Flathead men accompanied an overland fur brigade to St. Louis, Missouri. They sought a teacher who would instruct their people in the white man's religion. On reaching the famed river city they told their story to William Clark, superintendent in charge of all Indian affairs west of the Mississippi. He promised to help them, but actually did little. When their plea was printed in missionary magazines published in the East, it created a tremendous stir in church circles. Many yearned to convert the heathen savage to Christian ways. However, very few answered the call.

The only ones actually to settle in the Nez Percé country were Marcus and Narcissa Whitman and Henry and Eliza Spalding. In late 1836, the Whitmans established a mission at Waiilatpu, near present-day Walla Walla, Washington. But they ministered to a poor tribe, the Cayuse, who were distantly related to the Nez Percés. It was dour Henry and his frail Eliza who labored among the Nez Percés. Their small mission and school was established on Lapwai Creek, about twelve miles east of present-day Lewiston, Idaho. At first, both missionary couples reported many heathens were converted as the Indians eagerly accepted Christianity. Among those baptized by Reverend Spalding on November 17, 1839, were

Tuekakas and Asenoth, parents of several children. Tuekakas then changed his name to Joseph. Two boys born
later were also baptized and for a time attended the mission school. One was young Joseph, the other his brother
Ollokot who was two years younger. According to the
missionary, the father said his prayers faithfully and was
much attached to his Bible even though he could not read.

However, disappointment and disillusionment set in as
both missionary couples found themselves unable to
change their Indian charges over to the white man's way
of life. Marcus Whitman, a farm lad turned doctor and
missionary, was a tireless worker. Indeed, he had to be
in order to establish a self-supporting mission in the wilderness. He exhausted himself in raising crops and building dwellings for his family and few devoted charges.
Thus he could not swallow the Indians' dislike for farming. Vainly he tried to show them that by growing food
they need never suffer from hunger. But they wanted to
roam, instead of settling down, and did not wish to live
by the clock.

Both the Nez Percés and Cayuse were shocked and bitterly resentful when the missionaries ordered disobedient
adults whipped publicly as punishment for misdeeds. The
Cayuse allowed a husband to beat or even kill a bad wife,
but whipping was for horses! Then the missionaries tried
to teach them that horse-stealing, a highly developed and
popular skill, was wrong, and that killing their enemies
was bad, too. Relations became dangerously strained
after more missionaries arrived. They were a quarrel-
some, narrow-minded lot who unwisely tried to teach the
Indians that they were an inferior people, that they must
be ashamed of their "Indianness" and turn their backs on
their old ways.

The situation worsened further when wagon trains began arriving by the dozen. By this time the nation had "Oregon fever." Glowing tales of rich farmland and towering trees inspired thousands upon thousands to travel by covered wagon to Oregon. Some were able to purchase land from the Indians, particularly in central Oregon. But many settled down in whatever promising location pleased them. Often this was land claimed, by right of centuries of use, as tribal hunting grounds. This was especially true in the Cayuse territory where the newcomers were openly hostile to the natives and drove them away with threats and gunfire.

When the Cayuse contracted measles from immigrants who arrived late in 1847, many of their people died in spite of Dr. Whitman's efforts to save them. The Cayuse suspected the doctor was trying to poison them all so his white brothers could have the land to themselves. In retaliation, on November 29, 1847, they attacked the mission. They killed Dr. and Mrs. Whitman and twelve others. The Nez Percés took no part in this bloody uprising and escorted the Spaldings out of the country so they would not be harmed. After a white volunteer force from the Willamette Valley in Oregon punished the Cayuse, a peace of sorts settled over the region.

The peace did not last long there or elsewhere in the territories of Oregon and Washington. So many conflicts between Indians and whites flared up that in 1855, to avoid an all-out Indian war, Isaac I. Stevens, newly appointed governor of Washington Territory, invited all interested parties to come to Walla Walla late in May and air their complaints.

Such a council was not new. The pattern had been set

almost two hundred and fifty years earlier when Captain John Smith and other Jamestown settlers dickered with the chief of the Powhatan Confederacy in 1607. What happened at Walla Walla in 1855 and at later councils involving the Nez Percés was a repetition of happenings at other powwows resulting from the determined westward expansion of white people across Indian territory.

Governor Stevens was a well-educated, extremely able man in his late thirties. He had graduated from West Point, served with valor in the War with Mexico, and received scientific training with the United States Coast Survey. He organized a great survey of the entire West to determine the best route for a proposed transcontinental railroad. While he considered himself sympathetic toward Indians, he tolerated no opposition from them. He came to the council with prearranged plans to put all the upper Columbia and Snake River tribes on one huge reservation. His idea was not original because the government had treated the Indians living east of the Mississippi River similarly, by forcing them to leave their villages and settle in so-called Indian Territory, now the state of Oklahoma. Much to Governor Stevens' surprise he learned that this was impossible in the West. Some of the tribes were traditional enemies and could never live together peacefully. These included the Umatillas, Yakimas, Spokans, Nez Percés, Coeur d'Alenes, Walla Wallas, Palouse, Cayuse, and others.

To prepare for the council, an advance party erected tents, storehouses, and an outdoor arbor roofed with boughs. Twenty-five hundred Nez Percés arrived on May 24. The commissioners, who included Governor Stevens, his staff, and military aides, stepped out to greet them.

A photograph by Matthew Brady of Governor Isaac Stevens.

Among the chiefs were the elder Joseph and the elder Looking Glass. Here is how Governor Stevens described what followed: "A thousand warriors mounted on fine horses and riding at a gallop, two abreast, naked to the breech-clout, their faces covered with white, red, and yellow paint in fanciful designs, and decked with plumes and feathers and trinkets fluttering in the sunshine" came charging forward. They put on a great display of firing guns, riding, yelling, and brandishing war shields, and concluded with a war dance. The governor applauded the dazzling show. It never occurred to him that this was not meant as entertainment. It was the Nez Percés' way of showing their strength and courage. The other tribes made similar appearances so the actual council did not begin until May 29.

In the early afternoon, the participants gathered. The white leaders, wearing business suits and military uniforms, filed in and took their places on benches. Ranged behind them were armed soldiers, and to the side, a small group of half-breed and white interpreters. Then the chiefs appeared in full regalia and sat in the front row, facing the white officials. A thousand subchiefs, medicine men, and warriors gathered behind them. As each white man spoke, he could say only a few words. Then he must wait until these words were interpreted to various Indian criers, who translated loudly in tribal dialect to their people. The opening formalities dragged on until a downpour brought a postponement.

The next day, Governor Stevens made a long speech. To this day, historians cannot agree on whether he was stupid, two-faced, or wholly unaware of the Indian chiefs' intelligence. He spoke of the "long friendship" between the Great Father in Washington, D.C., and his red children. He said the Great Father wanted to do "something" for them.

The chiefs listened in stony silence. They knew what the Great Father had done to the Cherokees and Chickasaws and Iroquois and Sioux, to mention only a few once-powerful peoples. The chiefs knew that a white man's words could not be trusted and that he never kept the promises he made. However, many of those listening to the governor faced the inevitable. They knew their people were vastly outnumbered and must come to terms with the white man. They knew that the "something" the Great Father wanted to do for them was to have them surrender their freedom and live on a reservation *of the white man's choosing*.

When the governor finally sat down, the chiefs spoke in turn. Each described in great detail how kind and brave his people were, and how badly the settlers had treated them. The dickering then proceeded point by point, acre by acre, gift by gift, promise upon promise. The governor stressed two points: one, since many more white brothers were coming west, it was better for the Indians to sell portions of their hunting grounds to the government; two, it would be safer for them to live on a reservation because the soldiers would guarantee that no white men would be allowed to enter without their permission. But the bargaining lagged until the governor drew the boundaries for three separate reservations, one each for the Umatillas, the Yakimas, and the Nez Percés, and their cousins and allies. Then the bargaining resumed.

But the Nez Percés still argued that they could not sell the land, which was their mother. Gradually the governor, a skilled negotiator, brought about an acceptable "exchange" of money, the promise of a school, cattle, and annual donations of food and clothing. At this point Old Joseph asked for a guarantee that white men never would encroach on the reservation, which included the Wallowa Valley. The record shows that Governor Stevens stood before them "with hands uplifted just like a preacher" and vowed, "So long as water runs down to the ocean! So long as the sun travels across the sky shall this reservation belong to the Indians, and no white man shall be allowed on it." Thus reassured, Old Joseph and the other Nez Percé chiefs signed the written treaty placed before them. After the council concluded, the Indians returned to their homes. They were reasonably content with the reservation boundaries. The Nez Percé reserve was about 100 miles long and 60 miles wide and embraced all of the tribes' traditional campsites. All the Indians had been told that the treaty would not go into effect until Congress had ratified it.

Congress delayed *four years* before ratifying the Treaty of 1855 and cut back severely the money and goods promised the Nez Percés. Two more years passed before any payment was made. But meantime, only days after the great council disbanded, white men moved onto the land which the Indians had ceded to the government. "This is our land now," they said, driving the Indians away and seizing their horses and cattle. When the Indians appealed for help to Governor Stevens and the white agents placed in charge of their reservations, they were ignored.

One of the first valleys taken from the Nez Percés was the Grande Ronde in eastern Oregon. Adjoining it on the south across the deep canyon of the Grande Ronde River and snow-capped Wallowa Mountains was the Wallowa Valley, also called the Valley of Winding Waters. From the summit of the most accessible trail, Old Joseph watched the white settlers take over the Grande Ronde. As a precaution to discourage any who might prowl the heights in search of more green pastures, he had a line of poles driven across the trail into the Wallowa. This was his way of saying to the whites, *Keep Out*.

As late as the 1860's there was no road into the valley. The whites did stay away, but not because of the poles. Their attention was diverted elsewhere. A number of prospectors searching for gold had slipped onto the eastern portion of the Nez Percé reservation, which was in present-day Idaho. Their action was in deliberate defiance of the law. In late September of 1860, the members of a small party led by Elias D. Pierce camped on the bank of the North Fork of the Clearwater River (near present-day Pierce and Orofino). One man made a rich strike on a shallow tributary. As he whooped for joy, his companions swarmed over the stream and uncovered more gold. Pierce wrote later, "I never saw a party of men so much excited; they made the hills and mountains ring with shouts of joy."

Untroubled by the Indians, who were not interested in the yellow metal, the Pierce party washed out gold in pans and rockers until October 12. Then they returned to Walla Walla for the winter. The little settlement almost was turned upside down by the exciting news, which quickly carried down the Columbia River to The Dalles and Portland, then north to Puget Sound and south to California. By spring, fifteen thousand men were on their way to the Idaho discovery. Hasty negotiations with the

Nez Percé bands, whose hunting grounds were being over-run, resulted in their opening a corridor on the reservation as far south as the South Fork of the Clearwater River *for mining purposes only.*

As hordes of gold seekers poured in, settlements named Pierce and Orofino came into being. A wagon road connected them with another which also sprang up illegally on reservation land at the confluence of the Snake and Clearwater rivers. This was Lewiston, inland port for steamboats which made their way from Walla Walla with miners and supplies. Thus a wedge was driven into the heartland of the Nez Percé reservation. Ranchers and businessmen followed. Then the prospectors probed deeper and deeper into the mountain fastness where they had no right to enter and eventually discovered fabulously rich bonanzas of gold deep in the Salmon River country.

In vain the Nez Percés protested this unlawful invasion. Finally in 1863, government officials invited them to another council. This time the chiefs were urged to cede thousands of acres of their reservation to the government. Some were willing—but some were not. One cause of argument was the government's appointment of a chief named Lawyer to head all the Nez Percés, even though a number of the chiefs disliked him and refused to accept his actions as governing them. Then the government asked the chiefs to give up the Grande Ronde, the Wallowa, and Imnaha valleys to white settlement, even though none of them was gold country. However, the valleys were prime ranchland. Lawyer agreed, not only because he had been promised a house and cattle and liked his position of power, but also because this would not affect his people. Their traditional home was in the Clearwater drainage, already a part of the reservation. Naturally, Old Joseph, White Bird, Toolhoolhoolzote and several lesser chiefs objected. They refused to sign the Treaty of 1863 and withdrew to their remote valleys. It was at this point that the Nez Percés became divided into two groups: those who signed, and those who did not, or Treaty Nez Percés and non-Treaty Nez Percés.

But the dissenting chiefs did more than withdraw. By this time they were so bitter and so mistrustful, they totally rejected white customs, white neighbors, and Christianity. They threw away their Bibles, if they had them, and embraced the Dreamer faith. This was a new and peculiar religion they learned about through their contacts with the Columbia River tribes who also suffered from white men's depredations. Supposedly, the new belief began when a medicine man prophesied that some day the red man would rule the country again, conquer the whites and drive them out so the Indians could go back to living as their forefathers had. Basically, it was little different from the original primitive beliefs which the Nez Percés had held before they embraced Christianity. Since the medicine man foresaw in his dreams the victory of Indians over whites, his followers were called Dreamers. Because white men wore their hair cut short, and the missionaries made those Nez Percés who were Christian also cut theirs, the Dreamers let theirs grow again. They developed a sneering contempt for those bands who did sign the Treaty of 1863 and remained on the much-reduced reservation. Thus an unfortunate and deep breach developed, splitting the once-strong tribe into two factions.

IV   "Never sell the bones
of your father and mother"

In the summer of 1864, Old Joseph and his people watched from a distance as government surveyors charted a line through the Wallowa Valley. Since the surveyors did not bother the Indians and obviously were only camping, Old Joseph ignored them.

Here is how William H. Odell, the leader of the survey party, described the Wallowa Valley in his field journal. He wrote first that the valley was 6 miles wide and 40 miles long. "Narrow streams of clear cold water pour down from the high snowy mountains just to the South. Timber is to the South and West and along the banks of the streams. A large part of the valley is well adapted to agriculture, while the low grassy hills to the North and East furnish extensive range for stock. The finest of trout and salmon abound in the streams, and the surrounding mountains give evidence of plenty of game. Here I found many Indians camped upon the banks of the stream, taking great quantities of fish, while their large herds of horses quietly grazed on luxuriant grass. This valley should be surveyed as soon as practicable, for the wigwam of the savage will soon give way to the whites. Instead of the hunting and fishing grounds of the red men, the valley will teem with a thriving and busy population."

Perhaps it was just as well that Old Joseph never saw what Surveyor Odell wrote. But white men read it, particularly those in the United States General Land Office in Washington, D.C. The Wallowa Valley was marked for future settlement. The surveyors returned in 1865 and 1866, and laid out eleven townships. The Wallowas gave them no trouble.

By this time, Old Joseph was ailing and partially blind. Young Joseph was six feet two inches tall, handsome, with very large dark eyes, of gentle disposition, and very dignified. Ollokot was a gay, daring fellow, adept at hunting and fighting, and very popular with the warriors. Joseph, in contrast, was more closely attuned to the people. Both brothers now wore white men's trousers and Indian shirts and moccasins. They combed their dark hair back from the forehead in an unswept curl, gathering the rest in two braids. Both spoke a sort of part-English, part-Nez Percé jargon whenever they talked with white men, but relied on interpreters at councils.

In the spring of 1871, two white cattlemen married to Nez Percé women ventured into the Wallowa Valley with their cattle. They located homesteads along Hurricane Creek, far up the valley, and got along with the Wallowas.

In August of that year, Old Joseph told his sons: "You must stop your ears whenever you are asked to sign a treaty selling your home. A few years more, and white men will be all around you. They have their eyes on this land. My son, never forget my dying words. This country holds your father's body. Never sell the bones of your father and mother."

After the old man died, his grieving people built a fence around his grave. Within the enclosure they placed a pole topped by a bell which tolled in the wind. The early settlers respected the grave, but in 1874 a white man stole the bell. In 1886, the white rancher who owned the land dug up old Joseph's skull, boiled it clean, and put it on display in Baker, Oregon. The headless body was removed in 1926 to its present resting place at the foot of Wallowa Lake.

The people chose young Joseph as their leader. At this time he was 31, married, and father of a daughter. Being both gentle and wise, he did not become overly excited when the wagons of white settlers appeared on the hill overlooking the valley. But as more of them settled down in the Wallowa Valley, they seized the Indians' cattle and horses. They denied them the right to graze their stock, or tarry on ancient campsites, or even fish in the river. They mistreated and even killed some of the Indians. In spite of this, Joseph refused to allow his people to retaliate. Year in, year out, he strove to make friends with white families. He honestly believed the two could live side by side in peace.

By 1877, there were over eighty white ranches in the Wallowa Valley. In the early spring some of the settlers trumped up the false rumor that Joseph's band was plan-

General Oliver O. Howard, in a photograph taken by Matthew Brady.

ning to massacre them. In response to their cry for help, General Oliver O. Howard moved two companies of infantry into the valley, with orders to evict the Indians and force them to move onto the reservation.

General Howard had distinguished himself as a heroic military leader in the Civil War and had lost the lower portion of his right arm in battle. In September, 1874, he was named Commander of the Department of the Columbia for the United States Army. His headquarters were at Fort Vancouver on the lower Columbia River, in Washington Territory. From the moment he assumed his new duties, he faced an endless series of crises among the Indian tribes living in the vast area under his military jurisdiction. This area included Alaska, Washington, Oregon, and all of Idaho except its easternmost portion. Trouble bubbled up constantly. If the Indians were not fighting among themselves, they were harassing white settlers or gold miners. Thus his major problem was to settle the smaller disputes and avoid a major all-out Indian War.

From 1874 to the spring of 1877, General Howard made no concerted effort to force the non-Treaty Nez Percé bands to move onto their reservation. They were living peacefully in remote villages, and a capable man, John B. Monteith, was doing a good job as agent in charge of the reservation. But when the Wallowa Valley settlers called for help, the general decided that the time had come to deal firmly with the four chiefs, whom he considered renegades although none had given him any reason to label them as outlaws. By this time, however, he had become convinced that the only remaining obstacle to peaceful expansion of white settlers throughout the Pacific

Northwest was the Indian, and that the only way to maintain peace was to confine the natives to reservations where they could be kept under the watchful eye of the soldiers.

Of course, his thinking reflected that of General William Tecumseh Sherman, Commanding General of the United States Army, who was determined to whip all Indians so completely that they would never threaten or interfere with their conquerors then or in the future. In 1867, General Sherman phrased his policy on Indians in this way: "The more we can kill this year, the less will have to be killed in the next war, for the more I see of these Indians, the more convinced I am that they all have to be killed or be maintained as a species of paupers." Thus by 1877, the tribes of Washington Territory had been defeated and driven onto reservations, as well as the Klamaths and coastal tribes of Oregon, the Modocs of California, the Apaches, Comanches, and other plains tribes. Although the Sioux were still making trouble a year after the Custer massacre, the day of reckoning was closing in on them.

Thus, knowing his commander-in-chief's policies, there was no doubt in General Howard's mind as to what he was expected to do with the non-Treaty Nez Percés. So, in order to talk to the "malcontents," as he called them, he invited the Indian leaders to meet with him at Fort Lapwai in the first week in May. Looking Glass was not included, because his band lived on the reservation. Possibly because White Bird and Toolhoolhoolzote were elderly and Joseph was a strong, intelligent person, the general gained the impression that Joseph was the leader of the non-Treaty Indians and governed their actions. He was wrong, because at no time in the past or in the events to come was Joseph any more than chief of the Wallowa band.

Fortunately, we have Indian eyewitness accounts and the general's report of this council. Here is a greatly condensed scene, with the dialogue drawn from these sources.

After the opening ceremonies, Agent Monteith told the Indian leaders, "The law is, you must come to the reservation; the law is made in Washington."

General Howard, whom the Indians called Cut-Arm because of his battle injury, assured them, "The Government has set apart this large reservation for you and your children, that you may live in peace, and prosper."

Bristling old Toolhoolhoolzote said defiantly, through the interpreter, "What person pretends to divide the land, and put me on it?"

Apparently General Howard rose and, standing very straight, answered, "I am the man. I stand here for the President, and there is no spirit good or bad that will hinder me. My orders are plain, and will be executed. I hope that the Indians had good sense enough to make me their friend, and not their enemy." Then he delivered an ultimatum. He ordered all the non-Treaty Nez Percés to report to the reservation agency not later than June 14. The Indians protested vigorously that this did not give them time enough to round up their horses and cattle, and they would have to cross the Snake and Salmon rivers at flood-stage. General Howard thought they were making excuses, so he added, "If you let the time run over one day, the soldiers will be there to drive you onto the reservation, and all your cattle and horses outside of the reservation at that time will fall into the hands of the white men."

While General Howard was able to drive a hard bargain from his position of power, he did permit the chiefs to choose the sites where their people would settle. They selected the pleasant acres on the upper Clearwater River, near the village of Looking Glass.

The chiefs knew what had happened to the tribes in the Washington Territory, and others such as the Klamaths and Modocs. Small wonder they capitulated. Rather than have soldiers harming their families and white men grabbing their herds, Joseph, White Bird, and Toolhoolhoolzote agreed to give up their freedom and come onto the reservation by June 14. The original boundaries had been so reduced that they now encompassed an area about 30 miles wide and 45 miles deep, stretching from east of Lewiston to the west slope of the Bitterroot Mountains and southward through the Clearwater drainage to Grangeville.

When Joseph returned to his people and told them they had to move out of the Wallowa Valley, many burst into tears. The task was difficult. The ground was sodden from spring rain, the nights cold, the peaks hidden behind lowering clouds. Thousands of horses and cattle had to be rounded up. They floundered so in the mud that the cows with calves and mares with foals were left behind. Then the women dismantled the tepees, gathered up the tools, weapons, clothing, food, and ceremonial regalia, and packed these on the horses' backs. The tepee poles were used to make travois, or drags on which the old people and infants might travel. All would have to sleep out under the stars until they reached Tepahlewam.

After leaving the Wallowa Valley and crossing the lower adjoining Imnaha Valley, Joseph and his people trailed over a steep grassy divide and then descended to the bank of the Snake River. They moaned at the sight of the flood-swollen torrent. Joseph had tried in vain to convince General Howard that his people could not cross this wild river during its flood-stage. But the general insisted on the June 14 deadline, so there was nothing to do but prepare for the dangerous crossing. Some of the younger men eased their strongest horses into the water and found a firm fording. Meanwhile the men and women fashioned rafts or made bullboats of buffalo robes. On these were piled the elderly and infants, the baggage and dogs. Then with three or four ponies and strong men swimming alongside, the crude boats were pushed to the opposite shore. A few broke loose and bobbed downstream. A number of cattle and horses drowned. Somehow all the people made it to the far shore and dropped wearily on the grass. But after a rest, they pressed on up a steep draw and dropped down another slope to the Salmon River. It, too, was in flood. After crossing it, they struggled up a rocky canyon and finally came out onto the ancient rendezvous site at Tepahlewam. Here they were greeted by White Bird and Toolhoolhoolzote and their people and a few visitors from other bands.

And here, Wahlitits and his cousin brought down war on the people.

Labwai.

*A contemporary sketch by
Vincent Colyer of Fort Lapwai
as it looked at the time of the
Nez Percé campaign.*

V   The Battle in White Bird Canyon

The day Wahlitits and his companions went on their rampage was just another quiet day at Fort Lapwai, sixty miles to the north. The fort was situated on Lapwai Creek within the boundaries of the Nez Percé reservation. An aura of peace enveloped the small Army post, as soothing as the warm sun that bathed the empty parade ground. Most of the troopers were young, between eighteen and twenty-two, not too experienced in wilderness fighting, and not good marksmen. Nor were they given the opportunity to improve their skill, for the post commander, Captain David Perry, had a lackadaisical attitude toward handling firearms and practicing with live ammunition.

On June 14, the day the non-Treaty bands were to arrive on the reservation, Captain Perry rode to Lewiston to greet General Howard. He was coming to witness the arrival of the Indians, whom he mistrusted heartily. So the moment he and his aide stepped off the steamboat, he asked, "What about Joseph?"

Captain Perry assured him that, according to the best of his knowledge, Joseph and the non-Treaty Indians were on their way to the reservation. "They seem to be acting in good faith. They will make no trouble."

The general was satisfied. He knew Indians rarely met deadlines. As long as they were on their way to the agency and would report in a day or two, he would not send the soldiers to hurry them along.

However, that evening at Fort Lapwai after a dinner honoring the general, a courier arrived with a letter for Captain Perry. It was from L. P. Brown, a hotelkeeper at Mount Idaho, a hamlet very close to the rendezvous campsite. Mr. Brown wrote that the warriors had been observed going through the maneuvers of a fight. "They say openly they are going to fight the soldiers when they come up to put them on the reservation." This alarmed the citizens living near Mount Idaho and nearby Grangeville. The hotelkeeper advised, "I believe it would be well for you to send up, as soon as you can, a sufficient force to handle them without gloves, should they be disposed to resist. Sharp orders and prompt action will bring them to understand that they must comply with the orders of the government."

Captain Perry deferred to the general, who agreed the situation should be investigated. At dawn, a detachment of four men left Fort Lapwai. A good wagon road led up Lapwai Creek, over a pine-covered hill called Craig's Mountain, then down onto a nineteen-mile flat stretch called Camas Prairie to Mount Idaho. However, instead of going the full distance, the men returned at noon, their horses covered with lather. They were accompanied by two Treaty Indians who gave garbled details about some white ranchers having been killed.

Although none of the information implicated Joseph, the general immediately took it for granted that Joseph had started a war. But when the two officers rode over to talk with Mr. Monteith, the agent in charge of the reservation, he assured them it could not be true. The agent called in Whis-tas-ket, Joseph's father-in-law, who was a Treaty Indian. The old man said flatly, "Joseph would not fight." He and a companion left at once to contact Joseph and learn the full story. About four-thirty they returned on lathered horses, accompanied by two more Indians. One bore another message from Mr. Brown, the hotelkeeper, written at eight A.M. that morning. It confirmed the fact that the Nez Percé had killed several settlers. "One thing is certain. We are in the midst of an Indian war. . . . We want arms and ammunition and help at once. Don't delay a moment." The other Indian handed over another note which Brown had written an hour after his first one. It read: "Hurry up, hurry!"

The general dispatched his aide to ride to Fort Walla Walla with a request for additional troops and supplies. Meanwhile, Captain Perry prepared to march. At sunset, he and three junior officers led the two companies, totaling ninety-nine men, off to war. Each trooper was armed with a rifle and pistol, and forty rounds of ammunition. Their rations, field gear, and extra ammunition were loaded on five pack mules. Accompanying the small force were a half-breed interpreter and ten unarmed Treaty Indians whose mission was to urge Joseph not to fight.

Not long after they set out it began to rain. The troops sloshed through mud all night, covering forty miles. From daylight on they saw deserted ranches, some in smoking ruins, and a plundered freight wagon which had been delivering whiskey to Grangeville. About nine A.M., they came down off Craig's Mountain onto the Norton ranch, alongside Cottonwood Creek. The owner and his family were missing, and the house had been ransacked. The slower pack train finally arrived so the soldiers could cook bacon and coffee and receive their morning ration of bread. After the horses were watered and fed oats, the outfit marched another fifteen miles to Grangeville, arriving at sundown.

While the troops set up camp, Captain Perry conferred with the frightened citizens. They told him that many Indians had crossed Camas Prairie northeastward from their rendezvous. A few hours later the Indians were seen retracing their path. Now they were camped at the bottom of White Bird Canyon, only ten miles away.

The report was true. Joseph's band had hurried across the rolling prairie to join White Bird and his people, who had stopped to rest on lower Cottonwood Creek, about eight miles from the Norton ranch. After a council, the chiefs sent runners to the camp of Looking Glass, who lived nearby. However, Looking Glass flatly refused to join Joseph, White Bird, and Toolhoolhoolzote. He wanted no part of the war. The chiefs, disappointed, returned to the rendezvous site. Then, since the open terrain favored the kind of fighting white troops knew best, they continued southward to White Bird Creek. The creek, a tributary of the Salmon River, flowed through a canyon whose walls were two thousand feet deep, but covered with grass, rocks, and stunted trees.

There, the women raised the lodges, while the chiefs palavered with the warriors. No strategy was decided upon. Joseph insisted that he or his messengers be given the chance to parley with Army officers in a last effort to prevent a war. He maintained that if the people kept the peace and turned over the guilty renegades to the Army, the innocent ones would not be punished. They could resume their peaceful trek onto the reservation.

Back at Grangeville the settlers convinced Captain Perry that the only thing to do was to overtake the Indians before they crossed to the west bank of the Salmon and escaped into the rugged canyon country beyond. The captain agreed and asked for a guide. He also said he would welcome the assistance of citizen volunteers. Eleven settlers responded. One, Arthur or "Ad" Chapman, knew the countryside well enough to serve as a guide.

Chapman was a burly, talkative fellow who usually wore a big white hat. He was married to a Umatilla Indian and was disliked by both whites and Indians because of some questionable livestock deals. He appeared to be anxious to fight and assured Captain Perry that the non-Treaty Indians were cowards. Chapman described the lay of the land to him. White Bird Creek, he said, began

An artist's version of a Nez Percé attack on a wagon train.

near Grangeville and flowed down an ever-deepening canyon for ten miles before emptying into the Salmon River. The rim of the canyon sloped away over grass down to a long outcropping of rocks. The slope was steep, but not precipitous, and mounted horsemen could maneuver on it easily. The Indian camp was beyond and below the rocks. If the troops left quickly, Chapman said, they could be in good position along the rim of the canyon by midnight. At daylight they could sneak down and launch a surprise attack on the Indian camp while the people were sleeping.

Perry's men were weary and hungry. Some of the horses were so exhausted they lay down and refused their nosebag of oats. Nevertheless, the captain ordered his trumpeter to sound *"Boots and Saddles,"* the summons to mount and march forward under arms. The troops groaned, but saddled up. No effort was made to be quiet. Perhaps this mattered little since it is impossible to muffle the "march-walk" hoofbeats of over a hundred iron-shod horses. It was midnight when the troops halted at the canyon rim and dropped on the grass to await daylight. From the distance the soldiers heard a coyote's spine-tingling howl, but thought nothing of it. They should have. The "coyote" was a sentinel alerting the non-Treaty Indians that the soldiers were near their camp.

About two hours later, the light improved enough so the troops could saddle up. Through inefficiency or neglect, they were not ordered to cinch the saddle girths tightly before mounting. This mistake would cost them dearly later on. Slowly they eased onto the horse trail leading down into the canyon. A small detachment led by Lieutenant Edward R. Theller advanced with eight troopers, one of whom was Perry's trumpeter. Ad Chapman guided them. Whis-tas-ket and his friends tagged at the rear, in case a parley developed. When the lieutenant signaled he could see the Indian camp, the captain had his troops form a line at the trot.

Down below at the bottom of the canyon, the Indians spied the soldiers' advance. Immediately the warriors who were to form a truce team mounted the ponies tethered all night beside their tepees. War ponies were ridden only when they expected to fight. They moved away from camp bearing a white flag. Behind them came about seventy mounted warriors armed with bows and arrows, old cap-and-ball pistols, and a few hunting rifles.

Ad Chapman spotted the truce party first. Instead of allowing it to approach so a powwow that might have averted war could take place, he immediately fired on it. The truce team was not harmed, but one warrior took careful aim and killed the trumpeter riding next to Lieutenant Theller. Instantly a fight broke out on all sides. The warriors leaped on their ponies and swarmed up the slope.

Captain Perry was at an immediate disadvantage. His inexperienced troops were trained to respond to commands relayed through the trumpeter's piercing notes. Now he must use hand and hat signals which could hardly be seen through the dust boiling up on the canyonside. Still, he deployed his troops as best he could. The company in the center position dismounted and began firing. The other company on the right remained mounted. The civilian volunteers, quickly joined by Ad Chapman but not under his or any command, clustered atop some rocks. Lieutenant Theller's party attempted to pull back to a less-exposed position.

Unlike the soldiers, the warriors went into battle on their own and fought as they thought best. Thus some streaked toward the rocks, flinging shots and arrows at the volunteers, who promptly fled to Mount Idaho. Ollokot and his companions, including Wahlitits and Sarpsis Ilppilp, charged the mounted troops. The Army horses reared in fright and turned sharply to the rear. The saddles, which they had not cinched tightly enough earlier, slipped awry, frightening them more, and made it impossible for the riders to keep their seats. The Indians, yowling fiercely, soon put the cavalry force to rout. The men already on foot broke into squads and alternately fought and ran. Lieutenant Theller and his men made a valiant stand until everyone was killed.

Captain Perry reported later that panic soon extended to H troop, which disintegrated and melted away. From that time on, there was no organized fighting. The Indians chased the soldiers back thirteen miles as far as the Johnson ranch. There the captain managed to regroup his forces and made a desperate stand. Hours later, the warriors began to drop back gradually. Their firing died out as they returned to their camp. Now their prime concern was for their families, and how to best protect them from the next assault.

After a long, suspenseful wait, the captain led his troopers back to Grangeville. He sent word to Fort Lapwai of the humiliating defeat in White Bird Canyon. Roll call revealed Lieutenant Theller and thirty-three men were missing in action, but none of the survivors ventured out to retrieve the bodies until strong support arrived from the fort. When the squads did carry out their burial duties, they discovered no bodies scalped or mutilated, and no jewelry or watches taken. Only the soldiers' guns and ammunition had been appropriated.

The Indians reported to their chiefs, and the chiefs gave the word to the official camp crier. The crier went from lodge to lodge, calling out loudly so all could hear, that no warriors had been killed, only three were wounded slightly, and sixty-three rifles and ammunition had been gained. But instead of erupting in a victory celebration, the people were subdued and watchful.

In reporting the defeat to his superior officers and the newspapers in the region, General Howard inferred that the attacking force was led by Chief Joseph. In his white man's way of thinking, he could not imagine any attack being made without some advanced planning by a leader, a war chief. Thus Joseph, the only one who had insisted on a truce effort, became labeled as a wily fighting chief. It was easier for newspaper correspondents to use phrases such as "Joseph's warriors" or "Joseph's force" or "Joseph's strategy." Nothing could have been further from the truth. Chief Joseph had planned no advance strategy, nor had he led the attack. Although he acquitted himself well in the fighting, his was only one voice of several in the future councils. Other chiefs would direct the Indian campaign, but in the eyes of the American public, this was "Joseph's war."

*A painting by Paul Kane of a
Nez Percé brave, after a sketch
made by the artist on the
Columbia River.*

VI   The Attack on Looking Glass

Captain Perry's despatch brought near panic to Fort Lapwai and Lewiston. There were far too few troops in the area to put down an Indian uprising. General Howard speedily sent messages to Fort Walla Walla, Fort Vancouver, and San Francisco, asking for immediate troop reinforcements. Joseph was on the warpath, he told them.

Joseph . . . The name struck terror far and wide. In the region surrounding Fort Lapwai, families raced to the fort or Lewiston for protection. Others took refuge on islands in the rivers, raised stockades, and prepared to fight for their lives. In this mountain country where news was distributed by word-of-mouth, mounted riders sped to the most remote settlements. Miners dropped their tools, hurried down the rocky trails, and joined small forces behind barricades set up at crossroads stores. Groups of civilians formed volunteer companies, with the leaders and officers assuming military titles such as "Major" and "Captain." They set up drills and target practices and maintained guard watches day and night.

"Joseph is on the warpath!" the Treaty chiefs learned at the Lapwai agency store. They called their warriors and venerable old men to a council. Many were frightened because the non-Treaty Indians held them in contempt. Thus the rumor built up that Joseph and the warriors behind him might attack them. When Agent Monteith sent word that General Howard would pay for the services of any who served as scouts for the Army, over twenty hastened to enroll.

Where was Joseph during these suspenseful days? He, White Bird, Toolhoolhoolzote, and their people had crossed the swollen Salmon River and now were camped on the far bank about two miles below the mouth of White Bird Creek. Strategically it was an excellent position. Once their scouts figured out when more soldiers were approaching and what they might do, the people could move south, west, or north into rugged mountain country where they would have the military at a decided disadvantage. So, in spite of the widespread rumor that "Joseph" was pillaging far and wide, he and the others were waiting quietly beside the river for the Army to make another move.

When enough additional troops arrived to protect Lewiston and Fort Lapwai and bolster Captain Perry's bedraggled men, General Howard set out to make quick work of the non-Treaty Indians. His official report contains this colorful account of the leave-taking: "The cavalrymen set on their horses waiting the word; the infantry firmly grasping their rifles, are in line, ready to move; the artillery, who are really foot soldiers with a bright uniform, present their perfect ranks slightly retired from the rest. The mountain howitzer . . . and the two Gatling guns flank the picture on one side with their as yet restless, spirited animals. . . . The pack train, now an irregular body of noisy mules . . . remains grouped around the storehouse door. As I move out with my three staff officers, receive the salutes and listen to the firm, unhesitating manly orders that put the small mass in motion, a little of the old thrill of war comes back to me. . . . The cavalrymen led their horses, two abreast; the infantrymen followed, arms at ease, talking, smoking, and apparently lighthearted as boys on a holiday tramp. The mule column lumbered along . . . while the bell-mare kept up the unending ding-dong call."

Two days later, General Howard's force and the remnants of Perry's command camped on the Johnson Ranch, where Perry had made his desperate stand. The general immediately sent out squads to identify and bury the troopers killed in the battle of White Bird Canyon. He also sent a scouting detachment to locate Joseph. They didn't take long. The Indians were camped on a hillside across the river, in full view.

On Wednesday, June 27, Howard cautiously dispatched some troops to the bottom of the canyon. He and a company of artillery stayed up on the rim. In his field journal Howard wrote: "Joseph fighting chief. Indians are bold and waiting for us to engage them." Of the Nez Percé position across the river, he commented, "No general could have chosen a safer position, or one that would be more likely to puzzle and trouble a pursuing foe." He still thought of Joseph as a wily strategist, a "general." Actually, Joseph and the other chiefs were doing nothing more than watching the soldiers!

General Howard did exactly what the chiefs hoped he would. He gave orders for his troops to cross the river and attack the Indians. From his comfortable position on the rim of the canyon, the Salmon River looked like a mere creek. He fumed when preparations to cross dragged out through Wednesday, Thursday, and Friday. From a safe distance the Nez Percés watched with grim amusement the soldiers' attempts to cross. First, the mounted soldiers who tested for a fording almost drowned. Then there was a delay until small rowboats were obtained from ranchers. Efforts to row across failed. Next, two soldiers stripped down, looped a rope cable around their waists and swam across the two hundred yards of swift water. Another day was consumed in setting anchors on either bank and stretching the rope so a ferry could operate. But the pulley was too weak, and the current too strong. That failed. Finally, the strongest soldiers rowed skiffs across, with one poor fellow clinging to the rope. Although slow, this method succeeded.

Meanwhile, about noon on Thursday a number of Nez Percés, decked out in their finest war trappings, raced down the slope toward the riverbank. Neither their shots nor the soldiers' caused any casualties. Wahlitits and Sarpsis Ilppilp rode back and forth, brandishing guns and taunting the soldiers about being cowards. However, when one of the warriors saw artillerymen riding down the opposite slope with the big howitzer, the war party returned to their camp. The chiefs held another conference and agreed to allow the troops to cross the river without resisting them while the people withdrew higher into the hills. Their hope was to entice the soldiers into the mountains where they would be at a distinct disadvantage, and their horses would soon tire.

The move was not made until after dark. Imagine the difficulties of transporting tepees, household goods and food, the people, and two thousand ponies up onto a high rough mountainous plateau covered with a dense pine forest. Each chief looked after his own band as all moved twenty-five miles north toward a new position above a long-used ford of the Salmon River called Craig Billy's Crossing. They reached this point on July 1.

The morning after their departure, the Army officers trained their field glasses on the hillside. It was deserted! Or so they thought. They did not see the sentinels watching them from behind rocks, nor the warriors gathered behind a screen of pine trees. When an additional 175 troops arrived from Fort Lapwai, General Howard finally moved down to the banks of the Salmon River. Here he saw the powerful flood up close and realized why his men had had such difficulty in getting across. One wonders if he remembered that this was the *lesser* of the two swift rivers which he insisted Joseph and his people and their livestock cross.

Just before crossing on Friday, June 29, the general talked with some Treaty Nez Percés. They claimed that the non-Treaty chief, Looking Glass, had provided Joseph with forty fighting men and was also endangering the pack trains bringing supplies from Fort Lapwai. Very likely this false information was peddled by those who wanted to make trouble for Looking Glass. The general had no way of knowing it was untrue, nor did he have time to find out. Thereupon he committed the worst blunder of his conduct of the campaign. He ordered two companies under Captain Stephen G. Whipple to move out the next morning to arrest Looking Glass and all encamped with him.

The following account of what happened was taken from two sources: Peopeo Tholekt's narrative, written down by Mr. McWhorter, and an article published in the New York *Herald* on July 27, 1877. The latter was written by a newspaper correspondent named Thomas A. Sutherland. Twenty-seven years old, a graduate of Harvard University, and correspondent for the Portland (Oregon) *Standard,* the San Francisco *Chronicle,* and the New York *Herald,* he was the only professional newsman to follow the Nez Percé campaign to its bitter end. He camped with the general's officers.

Captain Whipple rode first to Mount Idaho where twenty civilians joined his troops. D. B. Randall offered to guide them to Looking Glass's village, which was at the junction of Clear Creek and the Middle Fork of the Clearwater River. It was very rough country, and the creek ran down through a fairly deep gulch. Midmorning on July 1, the troops reached the brow of the hill overlooking the village, which was located on the far side of the creek. The tepees were strung out on a grassy meadow. Behind them were fields planted to melons, potatoes, corn, and squash, and beyond them a herd of cattle grazed. There were about forty warriors and possibly a hundred and fifty elderly people, women, and children living there.

After the troops dismounted and the Gatling guns were placed to fire down on the village, Captain Whipple's men

Peopeo Tholekt, cousin of Chief Joseph. This photograph was taken by Delancey Gill in 1900, when Peopeo was about 39 years old.

and the volunteers spread out in a broad skirmish line. All moved cautiously down the slope. The Indians saw them and shouted the alarm. Looking Glass was eating in his tepee. He rushed out and, after one glance, sent Peopeo Tholekt to talk to them. "Tell them to leave us alone. We want no trouble."

The warrior climbed on his night pony, crossed the creek, and rode part way up the slope toward the soldiers. When they saw him they halted, and a small party of volunteers and soldiers moved forward to talk to him. Dutch Holmes, a volunteer, acted as interpreter. But before he could proceed, another volunteer jabbed his gun barrel into Peopeo Tholekt's ribs, and demanded: "You Looking Glass?"

"Hold on! This is not Looking Glass," Holmes exclaimed, restraining the man with difficulty. Then he told the Nez Percé to tell Looking Glass he must come out for a talk.

The chief and his people had watched the encounter and the way their man was threatened. Looking Glass sent the messenger and another warrior to raise a white flag halfway between his tepee and the creek and to invite the soldiers to come to the flag for a talk. This time the belligerent white man insisted the messenger was Looking Glass, and then tried to shoot him. Then Captain Whipple and several others rode over to the flag, while Peopeo Tholekt returned to the chief's tepee. Then a shot rang out, fired by another volunteer who had spied an Indian against whom he had a grudge. Fortunately the shot only wounded the Nez Percé in the ankle.

Captain Whipple and his party spurred their horses and bolted across the creek. The officer made no attempt to stop the barrage of shots unleashed by the soldiers against the village. Bullets tore into tepees and scoured the ground. The women grabbed their infants and small children and fled to the surrounding timber or across the Clearwater River. The warriors returned the fire until their families were out of rifle range. Then, realizing they were vastly outnumbered and facing artillery fire, they leaped on their ponies and made their escape. The soldiers and volunteers overran the village. They set fire to the tepees and food stores, bayoneted the prized copper kettles, trampled the gardens, and drove off seven hundred ponies and the cattle to Mount Idaho.

Long after the attackers had left, the Indians cautiously reappeared. Looking Glass was almost beside himself with anger at the unprovoked assault. Now he rejected his neutrality and vowed to join Joseph. Messengers left at once to locate the non-Treaty bands. Meanwhile, the women faced the sorrowful task of burying the dead and salvaging what little remained of their belongings.

Historians agree the attack was inexcusable. It drove to Joseph's support a warrior chief and his people who had wanted only peace. With them went another chief, Huishuis Kute, and his small band and a number of sympathizers from the Palouse tribe. When Captain Perry's force was defeated at White Bird Canyon, they faced about seventy warriors. Now the total of fighting men in the warrior camp would swell to over two hundred. Also, up to this moment, the non-Treaty Indians had no really effective war leader. White Bird and Toolhoolhoolzote were too old, and Joseph too gentle. But now Looking Glass was both eager and able and spoiling for revenge.

VII   Plenty Coups

When Captain Whipple returned to Mount Idaho, he found General Howard's ordnance officer awaiting him with a new order. The captain was told to move immediately back to the Norton ranch and await the pack train bringing supplies from Fort Lapwai. On arriving at the ranch, he had his men prepare defensive positions. The buildings were located near the head of Cottonwood Creek in an open ravine sheltered by wooded slopes on two sides and open to Camas Prairie on the others. To protect his camp against attack, he ordered four rifle pits dug on the slopes behind the buildings and a barricade of fence rails raised across the front.

Meantime, the Nez Percés had reached Craig Billy's Crossing of the Salmon River. They were confident that General Howard and his troops could not overtake them, for their scouts had reported that the soldiers were delayed atop a mountain by heavy fog and bad weather. Once more they crossed the swift river and set up camp on a flat area where the kouse grew in abundance. Now that acute danger was behind them, they laughed and sang as they set up housekeeping by the river. They were unaware that the soldiers were camped only ten miles to the east.

Some evidence exists that this river crossing was opposed by Chief Joseph. He wanted to retreat further into the Snake River heights and make a stand there. Instead, he was outvoted by the other chiefs who wanted to cross Camas Prairie and move into the equally rugged Clearwater country. The fact that there was dissent among the chiefs disproves General Howard's belief that Joseph was masterminding the Indian campaign.

On July 3, two young, inexperienced civilians named William Foster and Charles Blewett were sent by Captain Whipple to scout for Indians. They rode northeastward from the ranch over a high rolling ridge, then down across a small valley onto the southwest slope of Craig's Mountain. Here they suddenly encountered an Indian scout, Red Spy, who shot Blewett out of his saddle. Foster's shots went wild, and he beat a hasty retreat to the ranch, which was now called Cottonwood House. Captain Whipple quickly ordered Second Lieutenant Sevier M. Rains and ten cavalrymen to saddle up. Foster and another scout accompanied them. They hoped to rescue Blewett, if he was still alive.

Red Spy had chased Foster far enough to glimpse the soldiers' tents strung along Cottonwood Creek. He quickly returned to Blewett, who was dead. Still he struck him on the shoulder, because this was "counting coup," or signifying he had killed an enemy. After taking Blewett's gun, ammunition, and spyglass, he raced to the village. His news created great excitement among the warriors. They mounted hastily and followed him back to the place where he had killed Blewett. Soon they spied the military party approaching. According to Two Moons' account, the warriors dismounted and unwrapped their medicine packs, "objects wherein lay our strength," and put on the magic articles that would make them powerful fighters and protect them from death. They also sang their war songs in low tones as they hid in a small ravine nearby.

When the soldiers came close enough, the Indians attacked. Six soldiers were killed immediately. The others retreated behind some rocks, but they never had a chance. The warriors surrounded them and "counted coup" on the remaining seven. [A monument now marks the site.] Then the warriors began to argue; for some wanted to continue on and attack Whipple's camp. But Rainbow said they had accomplished enough for one day and talked them into returning to their own camp.

Not long after the Indians withdrew, Captain Whipple and his entire command came on the scene. When he saw the massacred men, he decided that his present position was much too perilous. Picking up Lieutenant Rains' body and leaving the rest exposed to the wolves and weather, he countermarched to Cottonwood House. The next morning, July 4, he rode out to meet the pack train and escorted it to the ranch. There Ad Chapman and five other civilians arrived to offer their services, and none too soon.

About noon, Indian ponies were seen on the hilltops above the rifle pits, but not a single Indian. After the ponies had spread out along the ridge top, riders suddenly leaped onto their backs and charged down the slope, yowling and shooting. The soldiers in the pits fired, and one squad trained the heavy Gatling gun on them. The Indians withdrew quickly and spent the rest of the day exchanging shots with their enemy, but from a safe distance. Nothing was accomplished by either side. However, some civilians did ride to Grangeville and recruit more men.

That night the chiefs, with Joseph dissenting, decided on a dangerous move. They struck camp very early the next morning, stringing out across Camas Prairie toward the South Fork of the Clearwater River. From there, if necessary, they would cross the Bitterroot Mountains and join the Crow Indians in eastern Montana. They figured (wrongly) that since the white men in Montana were not angry at them, they could settle on the buffalo range and live there in peace. Such a course of action was preferable to remaining in Idaho and fighting until the last man died. But to reach the Clearwater River, they must pass between the soldiers and the alarmed citizens of Grangeville. So, the main body of warriors rode with the people to protect them. At the same time, two scouting parties of about ten young warriors, including Wahlitits and Sarpsis Ilppilp, rode to the north, hoping to focus the attention of the soldiers on themselves while the people slipped by.

Meanwhile, seventeen civilians under "Captain" Randall, who had guided Whipple to Looking Glass's village, left Grangeville to assist the force at Cottonwood House. About four miles from their destination, they saw a large number of mounted Indians moving the pony herd across the prairie. Randall refused to turn back. He said that he had started for Cottonwood House and intended to reach it. His party pushed on, but soon saw the road ahead of them was blocked by a line of warriors. They had ridden right to the scouts.

"Hold up," Randall ordered. After some discussion, he and his companions decided to charge the line. They were well-armed with repeating rifles and rode fine horses.

Besides, they were only about two miles from Cottonwood House and assumed that if things got a little hot, the soldiers would rush to their rescue. All set their hats firmly and readied their guns. Then they rode toward the Indians at full gallop.

The warriors melted away on each side of the road and let the civilians pass. Then they slammed their heels into their ponies' flanks and rode up swiftly from the rear. One of the whites shouted the alarm. Randall glanced back and turned his horse off the road. He realized they could never make it to the ranch before being overrun. When the Indians started shooting, the first casualty was Randall's horse. As it stumbled, he shouted, "Don't run, boys! Let's fight!" By this time he and his companions had reached a slight elevation, where they foolishly dismounted to make a stand.

The sound of the shooting was heard plainly in the rifle pits behind the ranch house, a mile and a half away. Captain Perry, from his vantage point in one of the pits, is supposed to have remarked, "They cannot last a minute. They are goners." Then he continued watching for twenty-five minutes, without making any move to help.

Meantime, Randall was mortally wounded, but kept shooting until he died. Another man was killed outright, a third would die later of his wound, and a fourth was injured when his horse fell on him. After twenty-five minutes of blistering fighting, one man managed to escape the fighting and run to Cottonwood House. Captain Perry saw him approaching and went down to talk to him. When the man pleaded for help, the Captain offered only sympathy. He said he had to give up watching the fight, because it made him sick! Still, he refused to send troops to the rescue. He feared another repetition of what had happened in White Bird Canyon. The civilian gathered some ammunition and sped back to his comrades.

The fight, which had begun about eleven A.M., dragged on until mid-afternoon. During that time, the main body of Indians and their pony herd had run the dangerous gauntlet safely and were well across the prairie. The Indian scouts deliberately kept the fight going as long as they dared. When one of their number was killed, they slowly withdrew. Each one bragged Indian fashion that he had counted more coups than the others.

Not until the firing ceased did Captain Perry order twenty sharpshooters, under Captain Whipple, to ride out and assist the civilians. When the survivors returned to Grangeville to bury Randall, they told their story to Brown, the hotelkeeper. He wrote a scathing letter about the plight of "The Brave Seventeen" to Alonzo Leland, editor of *The Teller,* a newspaper published at Lewiston. He accused both Perry and Whipple of cowardice. "Our officers and men say that they learned the soldiers were anxious to go to the rescue, but were ordered back by the commanding officers. Time and time again they begged to go and were threatened with court-martial for disobedience of orders."

Captain Perry defended his conduct by saying that his mission was to guard the pack train. He felt the skirmish was some sort of trap to lure his troops into battle. Accusations flew hot and heavy on both sides. A military Court of Inquiry at Fort Lapwai heard the evidence and ruled that neither officer was guilty of improper conduct.

The day after the skirmish was July 6. That day Captain Perry finally got around to sending out a squad to

Camp on the Northern Pacific R.R.

Ft. Wal-lu-la on Columbia River.

*These impressions of the Nez Percé campaign were
published in the East in 1877.*

Nez Percés Boy and Papoose.

Perces.

Village of the Rovers.

bury the men, killed three days earlier, with Lieutenant Rains. The bodies were rolled into freshly-dug holes fifteen inches deep and covered with sod. [A plaque now marks the site.]

At this very time, ten miles further west, General Howard and his troops had reached the far shore of the Craig Billy's Crossing. Although the General knew the Nez Percés had forded at this point, he felt that a crossing was impossible. He wrote later: "The river is a perfect torrent." This left him with but one choice: retrace his route over the rugged mountains to the skiffs left anchored near shore at White Bird Crossing. By the time this was accomplished and the troops plodded up out of the steep canyon, the men were famished and exhausted. The rations were used up, and the pack train which would have supplied them was still pinned down at Cottonwood House.

General Howard had done just what the non-Treaty chiefs had hoped he would. He had floundered around through the mountains, worn out his men and horses, used up his supplies, and accomplished nothing. The civilians were highly critical of his performance as a commander, and their remarks were printed in newspapers all over the country. While the general's reputation suffered, that of the Indians improved considerably. Many settlers became openly contemptuous of the military bungling and praised Joseph for being a superb tactician. They called him a "red-skinned Napoleon Bonaparte."

The truth was quite the opposite. The Nez Percés had not yet rallied behind one strong leader, and when they did, it would not be Joseph.

VIII   The Battle of the Clearwater

As soon as the Nez Percés were far enough out on Camas Prairie not to be overtaken, the young warriors ranged far to the right and left of the column. That day and the next they raided about thirty ranches. Most were deserted, the owners having fled to Grangeville. Thus the renegades plundered freely, taking food and whatever else took their fancy, such as women's dresses and feathered hats, tablecloths, utensils, and even a rag doll. On July 7, they reached the edge of the prairie and streamed down a bluff to make camp at the confluence of Cottonwood Creek and the Clearwater River.

Quickly the tepees were raised, and the hunters sought fresh meat. The campsite was a poor choice as a defensive location because troops could approach the edge of the bluffs on either riverbank without being seen. Apparently the people were overconfident about having given the soldiers the slip. They did not even bother to post night guards. The next morning they had a moment of uneasiness when the hunters reported seeing dust rising to the north, for it could have meant that soldiers were approaching. However, the dust was raised by the movement of Looking Glass and Huishuis Kute and their bands. When they reached the camp, everyone exploded with frenzied excitement.

After the uproar subsided, the newcomers were treated to a hasty feast. Then everyone, young and old, gathered about a huge bonfire to hear Looking Glass tell about the attack on his village. The account was accompanied beforehand by much ceremony and lengthy oratory. Then each of the other chiefs rose to his feet and told how good and brave his people were, how badly they had been treated, and how they had outfought and outwitted Cut-Arm and his soldiers. But the climax of the evening came when Looking Glass announced that he would join the non-Treaty Indians in their war. The women shrieked, the drums began to throb, and the chiefs embraced Looking Glass. Hurriedly the singers and dancers donned their special regalia and led everyone in hours of dancing and whooping.

All this time the unhappy settlers in the Grangeville-Mount Idaho area reached the conclusion that if the Indian threat was to be wiped out, fearless civilians would have to do the job. The bumbling soldiers weren't accomplishing anything. Supremely confident in their prowess as fighters, forty-three of these volunteers organized themselves into a "regiment." They elected Ed McCon-

Looking Glass, mounted on a painted war horse. The photograph was taken in 1871, the year before Looking Glass was killed in battle.

ville as their leader and conferred on him the honorary rank of "Colonel." Finding horses enough to mount their war party was no problem. The men simply appropriated some of the ponies which had been trailed down from Looking Glass's village. On Sunday, July 8, with supplies on packhorses, the volunteers galloped off down a trail which paralleled the left, or west bank of the Clearwater River.

The river flowed northward through a narrow valley bounded on either side by steep pine-studded cliffs about one thousand feet high. Across the river on the east side, the cliff tops led onto rolling prairie deeply cut with ravines which were choked with trees and brush. In the late afternoon when the heights were still bathed in golden light but the valley was in blue shadow, McConville's men made camp. They were not aware that they were only about four miles south of the Nez Percé camp.

The civilians were saddle sore, covered with dust, their noses and necks sunburned. The spell of chilly, rainy weather had ended. Now the heat was so intense, they all perspired in their flannel shirts. While two of the party prepared a meal of bacon, potatoes, and coffee, the others unrolled their blankets and stacked their arms. Later McConville posted pickets a quarter, a half, and a full mile from camp, and guards around the horses. Knowing that the sound of voices carries farther at night when there is no wind, the men spoke softly as they relaxed about the campfire. By the time the stars came out, all but the guards were asleep.

About ten o'clock, the picket farthest out began hearing yips and yowls that could not be coyotes. Puzzled, he rode along the trail, stopping frequently to listen. About three miles further on, he emerged from some trees, and gasped. A half mile away was the Nez Percé camp. The Indians were having a rousing celebration.

After a long look, the man hastened back to alert McConville. "The Indians are close by, having a war dance!"

The "colonel" put on his boots, grabbed his rifle, and rode with the picket to the point where he could see the Indians. Since no sentinels challenged them, he figured rightly that the hostile Indians were overconfident now and saw no reason to keep their presence a secret. McConville returned to his camp, wakened the men, and conferred with "Captain" Cearly and "Lieutenant" Wilmot. "Let's hit the varmints with a surprise attack right now!" he urged.

As much as the other two relished a showdown, they advised caution. The canyon was not the most advantageous place for a small force to attack a large one. And, it would be better to wait until daylight and spy on the enemy before plunging into hasty action.

McConville finally agreed. He wrote a message to be delivered to General Howard, informing him of the location of the Nez Percés and promising to remain quiet until the Army moved up to attack. He also asked for reinforcements. After the messenger left, the volunteers snatched a little sleep until the first gray light of morning enabled them to tell a bush from a skulking Indian. They rode to the edge of the timber, left their horses, and spied on the Indian camp. Their throats turned dry as they counted more than two hundred fighting men and another five hundred women, children, and elderly people. They realized with thudding hearts what would have happened had they foolishly launched a surprise attack. Obviously the wise thing to do was to retire quietly and let the Army do battle.

Unfortunately, one man stumbled, and his rifle discharged. As the shot echoed throughout the canyon, the Indian camp buzzed like a hornet's nest. The volunteers sped back to their camp, grabbed their belongings, and moved to the summit of the nearest bluff. They had just thrown themselves on the ground to shoot when a large party of warriors appeared below. Ollokot, Rainbow, and Five Wounds led this force. After several hot exchanges of rifle fire, Ollokot realized there was only a small force atop the hill. He placed the best snipers in position to harass the white men and then withdrew with most of his comrades. The shooting continued all day Monday until about 9 P.M., when even the snipers ceased shooting.

McConville's men took advantage of the lull to heighten rock barricades, fill their canteens, and munch hardtack. Rest was impossible because the Indians returned at midnight and stole their horses. Now the volunteers were in truly desperate straits. Being outnumbered, they expected to be overrun the next day. Their only hope was to hold out until the troops galloped onto the scene.

At daylight the warriors resumed a lackadaisical shooting, just enough to keep the white men pinned down. Then they became bored and slipped away. Later in the afternoon about a dozen civilians arrived. They reported that General Howard had been delayed by the need to rest his troops and their mounts and to bring the pack train down from the fortified ranch on Cottonwood Creek. McConville cursed at the news and sent one man racing back to Grangeville to inform the general that his party desperately needed help.

The next morning, General Howard did get under way with six companies of infantry, five of artillery, and four of cavalry, in addition to his staff, scouts, fifty pack-train handlers, and several Treaty Indians. On the advice of Ad Chapman, the trigger-fingered, white-hatted civilian scout who had started the trouble at White Bird Canyon, the troops crossed the Clearwater River and proceeded along the east side. The high rolling prairie there was cut with numerous ravines, and in order to get around the head of them, Scout Chapman led the troops two miles back from the river. Thus they could not see the cliffs, the river, nor the hilltop where McConville's men were still pinned down by Indian fire.

On Tuesday evening the soldiers camped out on the prairie. Across the river McConville's men waited suspensefully for dark when they planned to make a break for Grangeville. And, since the Nez Percé scouts centered all their attention on this small group, there were no flankers across the river to warn of the Army's approach. Unaware of the mounting danger, the Indian families spent a pleasant evening visiting back and forth.

The next morning, the troops resumed their march. About 1 P.M. on this very hot Wednesday, Lieutenant Robert R. Fletcher and Ad Chapman, riding midway of the column, rode to the edge of the cliffs. They were astounded to discover the Indian camp across the river to their left. The women were cooking, the men lounging about, the children playing. Obviously they had no inkling of the trouble ahead.

Chapman quickly rode back to General Howard. The commander was so positive this was a camp of Treaty Indians that he did not halt the column. It proceeded on while he joined the lieutenant. A few Treaty Indians accompanied him and told him in no uncertain terms that he was looking down on the hostile camp. The general promptly ordered the howitzer and two Gatling guns brought to the rim, along with a company of infantry. Instead of retracing his path so this force would be directly opposite the Indian camp, he had the artillery fire from a distance. The cannon shot whistled over the camp and struck harmlessly onto the opposite slope. The infantrymen's bullets dropped like hail over the ravine at their feet.

The warriors immediately grabbed their weapons and raced for their ponies. Two groups moved to the outer edges of the encampment and prepared to defend the families, who were making hasty preparations to withdraw. The older boys moved the herd beyond reach of the shots. Tough old Toolhoolhoolzote leaped onto his pony and, yowling fiercely, led a charge across the river. His warriors rode part way up the slope, dismounted, and snaked up the ravine. Then they began firing from behind boulders and trees.

General Howard galloped back to the column which, by this time, had moved two miles north. Delay and confusion mounted as trumpeters relayed the calls to halt. The column finally turned around and rattled back to where the general was. There, some of the troopers piled their saddles in a semicircle barricade to form a headquarters of sorts from which he could conduct the battle.

The front line of infantry, fired upon by the warriors, toppled like tenpins. The inexperienced and inadequately trained men quavered at the sight of their companions dropping about them. They scurried for cover, but there was almost none on the grassy plain. Their shooting was wholly ineffective. The warriors shouted exuberantly to each other because they had stopped the troops from pouring down the slope onto their village.

The general rallied a second line of troops which charged toward the cliff edge. The Indians popped from behind their good cover, shot at them with deadly accuracy, and then ducked out of sight. These troops dropped back, dug rifle pits with their bayonets, and got set for a siege. Now the warriors who had held back to protect the village moved to support Toolhoolhoolzote. They very nearly captured the pack train and one field gun, but the troops fought so furiously that they were forced to retreat.

The battle raged on beneath the broiling sun, with the two lines of combatants facing each other from a distance of three hundred to six hundred yards. Since the village was not yet in danger, the people delayed their leaving, and the women brought water to the warriors on the slope. The wounded soldiers suffered for lack of it because the Indian sharpshooters kept their comrades from reaching the nearest spring.

Newspaperman Sutherland crept toward the front line so as to observe the fighting at close range. Every time he popped up for a look, the whine and thud of bullets singeing his hat made him hit the dirt. Still, he took notes on the desperate attempts by the Indians to capture the big guns and overwhelm the troopers.

While the general and his staff operated from behind a rampart of saddles, the chiefs gathered in a "smoking lodge." This was no more than some ground underneath an overhanging ledge of rock. The chiefs smoked while warriors brought in reports on the fighting and bragged about their deeds. When it was obvious the troops were pinned down, a number of warriors returned to the village. After several cannon balls exploded over the ravine, a few promptly quit fighting. This was their privilege. No chief had the right to force them to fight if they didn't want to.

As Roaring Eagle explained later: "We could not stand before the soldiers' big guns. We were forced back from that part of the field. The Indian way of fighting is not to get killed. Killed today, there can be no fighting tomorrow."

As darkness settled on Battle Ridge, as it was now called, there was little rest for either side. Warriors and troopers scuttled about, gathering in the wounded and improving their position. Fortunately, some soldiers located another spring and brought buckets of cool water to their thirsty comrades.

Of that first day's battle, General Howard wrote: "The Indians fought as well as any troops I ever saw and so did ours, not one man failing in duty." He does not mention that one hundred warriors kept over four hundred troops under siege all day and night. No doubt about it, the first twenty-four hours scored in favor of the Indians.

The second day was to be a costly setback for which the Nez Percés had only themselves to blame. The first day the warriors fought fiercely. The second day they gave up the fight. During the night, the chiefs and warriors quarreled about whether to stand and fight, or move the people to a more favorable location. The fighting strategy which they had learned from their fathers and grandfathers was to hit, slash, and run . . . as a wolf attacks his prey. It was not the Indian way to dig in and resist. So when the fighting resumed the next morning, some warriors refused to fight. Those who did fight grew angry at having to bear the full burden of the attack. But instead of fighting harder, or taunting the laggards into action, they gave up the fight too.

Thus, after the first hour of fighting, the soldiers noticed less shooting from the enemy. Alert to every development, General Howard sent word for everyone to get ready to charge. The moment the trumpet call sang out, the men roared, "To the river!" They jumped up and advanced while shooting. The few warriors left in the ravine below withdrew to the village.

As the first wave of troops appeared at the edge of the cliffs, the villagers sprang into action. Everyone started shrieking, grabbing, and running. Within moments all were in flight. However, since the soldiers found it very difficult to work down through the ravines, enough time elapsed for the Nez Percés to gather up a good part of their belongings before streaking up the heights and disappearing from sight. The slow-footed cattle were abandoned, but the horses were driven rapidly out of reach.

The canyon bottom was in shadow when the soldiers finally swarmed over the village. They raced about, setting fire to tepees and plundering the food supplies. Some held aloft silk dresses, and one brandished a rag doll. Most forgot about fighting in their zeal to collect souvenirs.

When General Howard reached the village, he was jubilant. He had scored an important victory, or so he thought. In his mind *Joseph* was defeated, and the hostile bands so dispersed that they could be rounded up easily and herded onto the reservation. Therefore he made another grievous blunder. He stopped fighting. He did not attempt to overtake the Indians. Historians feel that if Howard had pressed on, the war would have ended quickly in his favor.

Instead the general reasoned that with darkness coming on, the troops would lose themselves in the hills. Pursuit could wait. It was better to reorganize and count the cost of battle. The price was high: thirteen men killed and twenty-seven wounded. Nevertheless, he despatched messages to Fort Lapwai, announcing a stunning victory. The next day, he allowed his men to rest while the scouts ranged northward to locate the enemy.

The general would have been astounded had he known that the Nez Percés did not feel they had lost the Battle of the Clearwater. The chiefs and their people did not consider they had fled the scene. No, they had merely *withdrawn*, in true Indian defensive fashion. All through the night and next morning they pushed northward, until they came to an ancient fording ten miles downstream, near present-day Kamiah. Here they crossed the Clearwater River easily and continued to the top of the nearest heights. To catch them, the troops would have to approach up the long exposed slope, where they could be picked off by the Nez Percé sharpshooters. Although the bands had lost four warriors in the battle and left behind many possessions and much food, the warriors were still full of fight.

IX   The Lolo Trail

The next day, the Indians pushed on fifteen miles northeastward to Weippe Prairie. Here a non-Treaty band of twenty men, women, and children joined them. Their chief, Red Heart, explained that his people were returning from a buffalo hunt in Montana and were bound for their home ground at Kamiah. Looking Glass invited them to join the warring bands, but they refused. They wanted no part of war, so they left immediately for the Kamiah crossing of the Clearwater River. From there they hoped to move peacefully onto the reservation and "sit down" until the war was over. A few people from

Looking Glass's band joined them, raising their number to thirty-three.

By the time this band reached the Clearwater, General Howard's troops had advanced to the opposite shore. His Treaty Indian scouts identified Red Heart as a non-Treaty sympathizer. Although the chief and his people protested their innocence and declared they never had trouble with white people, General Howard ordered them all put under arrest. Their horses and equipment were seized, and the people marched, at an unnecessarily fast pace, sixty miles to Fort Lapwai. Here they were penned in a stockade under the broiling sun until August 4, when they were taken by steamboat far down the Columbia River to Fort Vancouver. Two months later they stood trial for "assisting Joseph," endured additional miserable imprisonment, and finally were released onto the Colville reservation in Eastern Washington. These were the only prisoners General Howard captured while he was in command of the fighting.

Indian scouts spying on the Army camp saw Red Heart's band seized. They sped back to Weippe Prairie with the news. The chiefs and leading warriors immediately gathered to decide what to do and where to go. Looking Glass argued forcefully for taking the high, difficult Lolo Trail to the buffalo grounds in Montana. The people there, he claimed, always treated the Nez Percés well when they crossed the Bitterroot Valley on their way east to the buffalo grounds along the lower Yellowstone River. Surely they would let their red brothers pass in peace. The Crows would welcome them and invite them to settle on the slopes of the mountains. After painting this rosy picture, Looking Glass concluded, "Listen to me, my chiefs. The Crows are the same as my brothers. If you go there with me, you will be safe."

Yellow Wolf asked, "What if the Crows do not welcome us?"

Looking Glass answered readily that then they could go north into Canada and join forces with the Sioux people, whose chief was Sitting Bull. There they would remain until "the trouble in Idaho blew away," and they could return to the land of their forefathers.

Each man who wished to speak did so because, as explained earlier, the Nez Percés firmly believed that the individual must be free to choose his own course of action. So now they were free to accept or reject Looking Glass's proposal and, if they wished, go their separate ways.

When Joseph's time came to speak, he launched into a long oration. He reminded the chiefs that he had never wanted war, but nevertheless had remained loyal to his brothers in their war. Cut-Arm (General Howard) had forced him and his people to leave their beloved Wallowa Valley. They had obeyed Cut-Arm's order only because they wanted peace and hoped some day to return there. But even while they camped at Tepahlewam, and Craig Billy's Crossing, and along Cottonwood Creek, they grieved at being separated from their homeland. Now Looking Glass wanted to lead them into exile, out of the land of their forefathers, out of Nez Percé country. Joseph said he was tired of running, running. He would rather stand and fight, even to death. "What are we fighting for, if not for our own country?" he demanded.

His speech swayed no one. White Bird, Toolhoolhoolzote, Huishuis Kute, and Hatalekin murmured acceptance of Looking Glass's proposal. Hatalekin was a Palouse

Indian who brought sixteen of his warriors to help the Nez Percés. White Bird spoke for this group, saying, "All right, Looking Glass. You take us to the Crow country."

Only Joseph and Ollokot voted against going into exile. The others accepted their objection without ill feeling and went on to the next order of business. They now had the problem of choosing a head chief to unify the withdrawal. A single command was something very new to Nez Percé custom and was considered only as a temporary measure. So, out of respect for their years, first Toolhoolhoolzote and then White Bird were offered the exalted position. Never before had one man assumed leadership of the non-Treaty Indians. The two aging chiefs declined the honor. They said they were too old to serve as war leader and recommended Looking Glass.

Joseph and Ollokot remained silent. Neither liked Looking Glass. They considered him overbearing, arrogant, and intolerant of other men's ideas. But to refuse to accompany the bands into exile and accept Looking Glass as head chief would mean that the Wallowa band must quit the protection of the warring bands and remain in Idaho. Here, because of their small number, they most certainly would be captured. The families would be mistreated and Joseph and Ollokot undoubtedly would be hanged. The brothers had a great horror of this form of white man's punishment and considered it unspeakably barbaric. Unlike the Indians of the eastern woodlands and the southwest, the Nez Percés killed their enemies swiftly. The prolonged agony of being choked to death was abhorrent to them. Thus, to protect their band and save their own necks, Joseph and Ollokot agreed to go into exile and to accept Looking Glass as their war leader.

But he would be *war* leader only. Each chief retained authority over his band in all other matters.

The council then adjourned so the chiefs might tell their people of the decision to go into exile. It is said the Wallowas wept like children. They were homesick for their snowy peaks and beautiful meadows. They did not want to leave unattended the graves of their forefathers and never again hear the bell tolling over Old Joseph's grave. Joseph got no rest that night as he tried to comfort his family and others. The old blind ones begged to be left behind so they could die in some place hidden from the soldiers. This was a time-honored custom chosen by the elderly, who saw nothing fearful about going into a long sleep in the arms of their mother, the earth. But Joseph asked them not to leave the families yet. So, in the very early morning they rose with the others and, in their faltering way, helped with the heartbreaking move into exile.

One wonders if the chiefs remembered that on this spot seventy-two years earlier their fathers had welcomed the starving men of the Lewis and Clark Expedition. The Nez Percés had been lords of the deep-canyon country then. Now they had lost almost everything except their horses. But of course, there was no time for reminiscing. Each chief counseled with the adults in his band. He stressed one point strongly: on the long trek to the buffalo grounds, none were to harass or shoot any white people, nor steal their livestock or belongings. As they had done for generations, they were to move peacefully across Montana.

Very early on the morning of July 16, 1877, the Nez Percés abandoned Weippe Prairie. They still numbered over two hundred and fifty fighting men and five hundred women and children. They drove a herd of about two thousand ponies and pack animals. Soon they approached steep wooded foothills and began the long difficult climb to the summit of the trail over the extremely rugged mountains. The route was well-marked because it had been used for centuries.

Later, careless writers and artists would picture the Nez Percés trailing cattle over the divide and using travois, or skins stretched between long poles, to transport their baggage. Such descriptions were inaccurate, for by this time the Nez Percés had no cattle left, and travois could not be used on such rocky and precipitous ground. The feeble elderly folk and youngest children rode on the most dependable ponies.

Five of the younger warriors, including Wahlitits and Sarpsis Ilppilp, remained at Weippe Prairie as a rear guard. They divided among themselves the dangerous tasks of spying on the soldiers and keeping their people informed. As soon as the bands were out of sight, the warriors hid at the edge of the timber enclosing the first segment of the Lolo Trail. From their vantage point they had an excellent view of the full sweep of Weippe Prairie.

Meantime General Howard finally was getting into action again. He dispatched four companies of cavalry to cross the Clearwater and pursue the fleeing bands. With them went McConville's volunteers, Ad Chapman, who now served as chief of scouts, and some Treaty Nez Percés. Perhaps the latter wished to ingratiate themselves with the white soldiers. Perhaps they were jealous of Joseph or of Looking Glass. At any rate, they were willing to accept pay for working against their own people. Actually their scouting assistance was not needed. The trail was clear because it is impossible to move seven hundred people and two thousand horses overland without leaving considerable evidence.

By midafternoon of July 16, the military force came into the sight of the warriors hidden in the forest. Immediately Wahlitits leaped on his pony and sped to warn Looking Glass. Sixteen warriors, including Rainbow and Two Moons, returned to support the rear guard. All hid themselves behind the dense undergrowth as the enemy column came closer and closer. The scouts rode at the head, followed by the volunteers, and the troops two miles to the rear. When Major Edward C. Mason, who was in command, was told the trail led into the thick stand of timber, he halted the column. After a discussion, he ordered the scouts and volunteers to move ahead cautiously.

Here is Two Moons' account of what happened: "We hid in the brush to get them at close range. Soon the voices grew. Several men were drawing near. It was the language we understood. We then knew they were Nez Percé scouts. Christians of our tribe, working for the Government against their own tribe, their own blood people! They came into our sight and were looking at the trackprints of horses. Rainbow took a shot and wounded one of them."

Rainbow fired too soon. Had he waited until the entire command was drawn into the timber, he and the warriors could have inflicted terrible damage on their enemy. The disaster could have been more costly than the encounter at White Bird Canyon. Instead, Rainbow's shot sent the scouts fleeing in haste. One of their number lay dead, and two others had received mortal wounds. The frightened

In pursuit of Jo

Indians immediately rode back to McConville's men, who joined them in full retreat to Mason's command. After a lengthy delay, the major ordered everyone back to the main camp on the Clearwater.

Incredible as it seems, General Howard dillydallied in camp for nearly two more weeks. He thought up one plan of pursuit, scrapped it, and devised another. Then he

A contemporary sketch of a scene from the Nez Percé campaign.

waited for reinforcements and supplies and recruited a crew of fifty civilian axemen to clear the trail. He alerted the commander of tiny Fort Missoula in Montana Territory to "engage" the fleeing Nez Percés until he, Howard, could arrive and subdue them. Once the Nez Percés crossed the divide into Montana, they were outside General Howard's command. But when he sent a telegraph message to General Sherman, Commanding General of the Army, that seven hundred Indians were on the "warpath," General Sherman ordered him to continue the pursuit beyond the boundaries of his authority.

During this period the Nez Percés crossed the torturous Lolo Trail. Progress was slow because in many places the trees grew so closely together that the heavily laden packhorses got stuck. A steady rain churned the trail to glassy mud. The passage through spruce, cedar, and pine trees was gloomy and twisting. On more than one segment a breath-holding caution was needed in picking the way across treacherous slide rock. The Indians traveled in family groups, each looking after itself on the trail and at night, when it was necessary to drop beside the road to sleep. For much of the journey, the timber was too tangled for hunting. But the people did not go hungry. Every one on foot gathered berries, or roots, or scraped the inner bark from certain shrubs. The hunters who ranged ahead brought down elk and deer in the high meadows and trimmed them out so there was fresh meat readily available. The hides were scraped for future clothing, and the entrails thrown to the ravenous dogs.

Nine days later, the people began their descent of the east slope of the Bitterroot Mountains. On that day, General Howard set forth on what he described as "hot pursuit of the hostiles."

X   The Battle of the Big Hole

Residents of western Montana read newspaper accounts of the Nez Percé conflict and knew the warring bands were headed in their direction. At first they viewed the news calmly. The Nez Percés had moved back and forth across the mountain-rimmed Bitterroot Valley for generations in their journeys to and from the buffalo hunting grounds. Because the Indians were friendly and likeable, the residents did not bother them. In fact, merchants treated them well when they appeared in the stores, because they paid in currency or gold dust received from the sale of their horses. Since the local Indians, the Flatheads, were peaceful, the Indian situation in western Montana was stable.

But when General Howard telegraphed Captain Charles C. Rawn, the officer in charge of Fort Missoula, to intercept the Nez Percés when they emerged from the Lolo Trail, some Montanans became alarmed. From the way the newspapers whooped up the news and lavished much detail on the gory deeds of Wahlitits and his comrades, citizens feared that a vast number of bloodthirsty Indians were about to descend on them. Bankers, clerks, cowboys, and miners flocked together to drill and practice riflery. More than a hundred volunteered to assist Rawn's tiny force. Schools closed, and women and children took refuge in the larger homes where they could be protected more easily. Even the harmless Indian beggars who lived near the small town dumps were clapped into jail and accused of plotting against the whites. As the hysteria mounted, Governor Benjamin F. Potts issued a call for more volunteers. *The Weekly Missoulian* did not help when it ran a bold headline that read: "Help! Help! Come running!"

Meantime, Colonel John Gibbon, commandant at Fort Shaw, also received orders to move out and engage the Nez Percés. He promptly gathered up seventeen officers, 146 enlisted men of the Seventh Infantry, a mounted cannon, and long pack train, and marched southwest toward the Bitterroot.

By July 24, Captain Rawn reached a position six miles above the mouth of Lolo Creek with his five officers and thirty enlisted men. Soon they were joined by two hundred volunteers staggering under the weight of an assortment of weapons. The next day they began building a barricade of logs, which resembled a large corral. The walls were only three logs high when a peace party of Nez Percés, mounted and carrying a white flag, emerged from the dense timber onto a meadow beside Lolo Creek. The soldiers lunged for their rifles and took defensive positions. But many of the volunteers, long-time residents of the Bitterroot Valley, were not alarmed. They recognized the peace party members as being Looking Glass, White Bird, and Joseph. The three halted at a distance and waited for a delegation to come out to parley. When the white delegation arrived, the chiefs told them that they wished to pass peacefully across the valley on their way to the buffalo grounds. They would behave as Nez Percés had for decades. In other words, they would harm no one.

Captain Rawn answered that they could do so, but only if they first surrendered all their arms. The chiefs refused. White Bird recalled the time in 1858, when the Yakimas and Spokans were in a similar situation and had agreed to surrender their arms. When they did so on the promise of not being bothered, they were seized. Some were imprisoned, and several were hanged. Thus White Bird was not going to accept what he felt was a trap. Looking Glass reminded the captain that no Nez Percé could believe anything a white man said. There is no record of what Joseph might have contributed to the parley. The captain suggested the two parties meet again the following day to discuss the matter further. He was stalling for time, hoping Colonel Gibbon would arrive to "handle" the Indians.

The next parley, on June 26, accomplished nothing, as Captain Rawn intended, and a third meeting was arranged for the following morning. But by this time most of the civilians believed the Nez Percés were not dangerous and went home. The Nez Percés rose very early the next morning, climbed from the creek to the heights with their baggage and horses, circumvented the armed men in the barricade, and moved on without difficulty to the valley. Captain Rawn had no choice but to move his force down to the mouth of Lolo Creek and await Colonel Gibbon. When Montanans learned how the Nez Percés had outwitted the soldiers, they dubbed the corral Fort Fizzle. [It was used for years to hold stock, but burned in 1934. Now the site is marked with one of Montana's large and handsome historical markers.]

Looking Glass made much of the fact that the people had no trouble moving across the valley and on up the steep eastern slope. Just as he had said, the Montanans were friendly. This made him over-confident, and he allowed the weary families to dawdle along. He assured them the war was behind them, even though friendly ranchers warned him a large military force was on its way to overtake them.

At this time, a half-French, half-Nez Percé hunter named Poker Joe offered to guide the people through the mountains. The Nez Percés didn't think they needed his services, but welcomed him anyway. All went well for a few days. Everyone except the homesick Wallowas was happy. They shrugged off the losses of the battle on the Clearwater and looked forward to the reunion with their friends, the Crows. The hunters brought in much meat, the women found camas to dig and fish in the creeks, and the ponies grazed on the lush grass. Soon the people attained the heights and looked down on the Big Hole Basin. It is a magnificently beautiful valley, 6,800 feet high and about 60 miles long, literally a "big hole" in the mountains. The slopes glowed with wildflowers, and the willows along the silvery creeks housed thousands of songbirds. The native nut grass on the valley floor supported large herds of elk, deer, and buffalo.

There was one disturbing note, however. The night before, Wahlitits had had a bad dream. In the morning he rode among the people shouting what he had dreamed and announcing, "I will be killed soon. . . . We are all going to die!" Then other warriors admitted that they, too, had had bad dreams. They urged Looking Glass to "hurry, hurry up" because "death is following on our trail." But the supremely confident Looking Glass scoffed at them and called them cowards.

On August 7, the people streamed down the slope and reached a meadow beside the clear, swift Big Hole River. Here all went into camp. Looking Glass felt so secure that he did not even post guards around the herd, nor back along the trail. Some of the warriors protested and tried to borrow fast horses in order to search back over the heights. The war chief refused their request. They accepted his decision, but one named Five Wounds warned, "Whatever the loss, it is yours." In view of what happened shortly after, it is surprising that some of these warriors did not slip out secretly and scout on their own. If they had, they would have observed the soldiers approaching. Regrettably they did nothing.

That night the fires blazed brightly, and the people sang and danced. The next day the warriors went hunting again, while the women cut new lodge poles and dug more camas. The bulbs were set to baking in a huge pit covered with dirt and glowing coals. The older women busied themselves cleaning and curing the hides accumulated during the journey because already some families needed moccasins. Again there was dancing by starlight, and it was late before the people withdrew to their tepees.

During this time, Colonel Gibbon's force had reached the Bitterroot Valley, where they were joined by Captain Rawn's command. A company of thirty-four civilians headed by John B. Catlin volunteered their services on being told that after the Indians were whipped in the battle that was shaping up, they might divide the pony herd among themselves. Since horses were in great demand on the frontier and were dubbed "walking wealth," the volunteers cheered. They seemed to have forgotten that only a few days before they had quit Fort Fizzle so their old-time Nez Percé friends could continue on across the valley without having to fight a running battle.

Gibbon marched this strong command rapidly toward the Big Hole, advancing twice as many miles per day as the Indians had. Catlin's men scouted ahead and soon determined that the Nez Percés were camped at the foot of the east slope of the mountains. By nightfall of August 7, the troops topped the broad forested summit and hid themselves in the trees.

After a conference, Lieutenant James H. Bradley, who had gained valuable experience fighting the Sioux, set forth with a guide, thirty soldiers, and all the volunteers. This detachment picked its way across the mountain top. Shortly after daylight the men heard the sounds of axes and women's voices. One man shinnied up a tall pine tree, spied the women cutting lodge poles, and saw the camp at the confluence of the river and creek. He counted eighty-nine tepees lined out in a V formation along the banks of both streams. When Lieutenant Bradley learned this, he ordered his men to hide themselves while a messenger raced back to Colonel Gibbon. That officer advanced as quickly and quietly as possible, leaving behind

A pack train carries supplies to the Army over the Dead Mule Trail in Idaho. From a sketch by an Army officer.

the pack train, howitzer, horses, and wagons. These would move forward only after the troops were engaged in battle.

By the time Gibbon's command joined those hidden at the rim of the slope, it was dark. Nevertheless, the men strung out along a twelve-hundred-yard skirmish line. Very cautiously, one quiet step at a time, they began to ease down the wooded slope. Suddenly they froze. Over the clean fragrance of piney woods they smelled horse-flesh. They had reached the pony herd. After a long pause they inched by so slowly that the animals, instead of snorting in alarm, drifted higher on the slope and resumed grazing. Now any Indians hoping to flee must run through the soldiers' line.

After midnight the line halted, and the men stretched out on the ground to rest. By four A.M., the light had improved enough so all could look down on the Indian camp. Colonel Gibbon and his staff held a whispered conference. The left wing of the line was placed in command of Lieutenant Bradley, and included the civilians. It was to strike the northernmost tepees. Two companies of infantry would hit the center of the village. Captain William Logan and his infantrymen were to attack the southern portion of the camp. The plan was to force the Indians out of the village and onto the treeless valley floor. There, far removed from their horses, they could be run down and overwhelmed. Captain Rawn's men were told to stay on the slope as a reserve force. A squad moved off to work the pony herd farther up the slope, well out of reach of the owners.

Before the war conference broke up, Mr. Catlin asked Colonel Gibbon if they should try to capture any of the

Indians and hold them prisoner. Gibbon is supposed to have shaken his head and replied that he had come to do only one thing: *kill.*

The fighters eased forward through the timber until they were only two hundred yards from the camp. Then they saw an elderly Indian emerge from a tepee, mount the night pony tethered alongside, and head toward them. Obviously he was checking on the pony herd. Because he was half blind, he did not make out the soldiers even when he saw figures loom up in front of him. The volunteers shot first, riddling him with bullets. On command, the troops fired three volleys into the tepees. Then, shouting fiercely, they charged left, center, and right positions.

As the shots ripped through the tepees, the warriors bounded to their feet and grabbed their weapons. The women gathered up the children and rushed, screaming, from the lodges. Many were caught in a volley of shots and crumpled. But the soldiers who charged the village came up against the warriors' guns and arrows and suffered casualties. Many engaged in hand-to-hand fighting. They had expected a swift, hot skirmish and immediate routing of the enemy. Instead they were caught in a terrible fight to the death. Bullets and arrows streaked in every direction. As bodies slumped to the ground, the grass was drenched with blood.

Here is how an Indian, Wounded Head, described the battle: "The sound of the guns awoke most of the band, and the battle took place. Hand to hand, club to club. All mixed up, warriors and soldiers fought. It was a bloody battle." The ten-year-old nephew of White Bird recalled: "Indians war-whooping, soldiers yelling, driving through the brush, hunting out Indians." After a pause, the youngster added stoutly: "Was not scared."

Two Moons said: "Bullets were singing through the tepee, splintering the poles. They came thick like the summer hail for a time, and I did not dare raise up. Shouts and war whoops mingled with the firing. Children and women crying. At last I sprang up, got my rifle from the pole and rushed out to meet the soldiers. . . . Then did the soldiers fire at me, bullets falling as the acorns in the autumn winds."

The village was strung out too much for the military line to contain it. One of the first casualties was Lieutenant Bradley. His leaderless men floundered about and did not press their attack. This opened an area through which the Indian families could escape. While most warriors fought savagely, some carried out their first obligation, which was to assist the families. This was Joseph and White Bird's sacred trust. They and their helpers gathered up infants, toddlers, and wounded mothers and helped them hide in the willows near the river. Time and time again they dodged the soldiers' bullets in order to aid the people. Those already injured hobbled or crawled away. Gradually the Indian attack intensified, and the troops were forced back up the slope. The younger fighters climbed trees in order to pick off the soldiers with deadly accuracy. One by one, they were shot out of their exposed positions.

By this time, Colonel Gibbon had realized that fighting "by the book" was useless. Somehow in all the horrible din, the trumpeter's shrill notes relayed his new commands. The men began withdrawing up the slope in greater numbers. Here they dug in behind trees and boulders and gradually formed a square. Seeing this, the warriors whooped up a new attack and beseiged them with shots from all sides.

As soon as the children were hidden safely, the women crept back to the village to rescue the wounded and drag off the dead. They found thirty dead in the slashed and smouldering tepees and twenty more along the creek or river. One of these was Wahlitits. His wife was also dead. Another was Hatalekin, the Palouse warrior. Still another was Rainbow, a greatly loved man who drew his power from the sky. When the word was shouted that Rainbow was dead, Five Wounds stopped fighting. He dropped his bow and cried.

All that day, the younger warriors pressed their siege. They kept the soldiers pinned down so the family men could retire to move the people to a safer place. Joseph and his helpers managed to reach the herd, turn it, and bring it back close enough so many of the ponies could be loaded with belongings. Then he supervised the sad task of seeing that the dead were hastily buried. One of them was his older wife. But this time there was no time to paint the faces of the dead ones, or slip the copper wire bracelets from their arms, and bury them deeply with appropriate prayers and chants. The burials were hasty, the graves shallow. Meantime the women salvaged as many tepee poles and hides as possible, fashioned travois, and loaded them. By early afternoon the people were on their way southward. But they stayed close to the sheltering trees along the western edge of the basin.

About this time, they spied the soldiers coming down the slope with the howitzer and extra ammunition. The warriors nearest them rushed to attack. The soldiers fired the big gun twice, inflicting no damage, and then fled.

Peopeo Tholekt led the attack. He dismantled the gun and hid the barrel in the brush. The others pounced on the ammunition mule and removed two thousand rifle cartridges. These they carried back to the other warriors, along with Springfield rifles taken from the dead soldiers.

Both whites and Indians suffered more casualties that afternoon. One of the latter was Sarpsis Ilppilp, who had joined Wahlitits in the bloody raid that started the war. Then Five Wounds, who had mourned loudly for his friend Rainbow, apparently decided he did not want to live any longer. He stood up in full view of the soldiers and asked them to kill him. They did. Those near by claim they saw his spirit leap from his body and join that of Rainbow's.

As darkness settled over the basin and smoke from the burning village blanketed the battlefield, more warriors withdrew. But Ollokot and his comrades continued the siege all night so the families could pull farther and farther away. They could hear the soldiers calling for water, and the wounded crying in pain. By scuttling about in the darkness on all sides, they prevented the enemy from getting any rest. However, two soldiers volunteered for the dangerous task of carrying a message for help. A small miracle occurred when a civilian crept *into* the camp, right under the noses of the warriors, and brought the glad news that General Howard was coming on the double. This so encouraged the remaining able men that they set to with renewed vigor to deepen the trenches.

At daybreak the warriors started firing rapidly. The soldiers braced for trouble, but the shots were only a last contemptuous gesture from the Indians. They withdrew to the ponies left for them in the willows nearby and raced to join their people. The soldiers did not try to follow. When General Howard finally arrived the next morning, he found many in a state of shock, sitting disconsolately by the graves of their companions. The cost of the battle had been high: twenty-nine soldiers and civilians dead, including seven officers, and forty-two wounded, most seriously. Later, Colonel Gibbon would be severely criticized for the brutal way some of his men treated the defenseless Indian women and children. But this could not offset the fact that the soldiers and civilians had fought very bravely.

[Today the battlefield is a well-maintained National Monument. In spite of its remote location, thousands of tourists visit it annually. They walk between the old trenches and bullet-scarred trees and read the plaques on the monuments raised in memory of both whites and Indians. In the attractive museum they can hear a recorded story of the Battle of the Big Hole.]

No one, neither white nor red, could say positively how many Nez Percés died during the battle. The total varied from sixty to ninety, of whom many were women and children. But there is no doubt that twelve of the best warriors were killed. Their loss was a crushing blow to the Nez Percés. The mourning, in true Indian fashion, was loud and piteous, but it was cruelly short. For the rest of their lives, some of the people worried about whether the spirits of the fallen ones floated freely in the sky because the bodies had not been properly buried. No one talked about the lost ones having gone to the "happy hunting grounds." This was a white man's expression rejected by all Indians.

Not only the dead were mourned. The people grieved

because they had recognized old friends from the Bitterroot Valley fighting alongside the soldiers. At this point, Joseph finally gave up hoping that his people ever could dwell in peaceful neighborliness with white settlers. From this day on he never raised his voice to criticize the wildly bitter warriors. Now all boiled with revenge and would kill and pillage as their families fled like hunted animals across Montana toward Yellowstone National Park.

Looking Glass found himself totally disgraced. All blamed him for the tragedy because he had allowed the people to dawdle. They rejected him as their war leader. However, when the chiefs joined in council to decide what to do next, Looking Glass was included. This was his privilege, since he remained chief of his band. Now there was little argument. All agreed their only chance for survival lay in fleeing to Canada, where the Americans would not dare touch them. So they chose as their new leader the man who best knew the way to Canada. He was not Joseph, nor any other chief, but the able half-breed Poker Joe.

Wottolen said of the new leader: "He had been all over that country, east and north, and he knew the land and the trails. He understood, and would have the people up early in the morning, and travel till about ten o'clock. Then he ordered a stop and cooking was done while the horses filled up on grass. About two o'clock he would travel again. Kept going until about ten o'clock at night. We had no timepiece, but we could easily judge our movements. In this way the people covered many miles each sun."

XI   A Night Raid at Camas Meadows

The Nez Percés outdistanced the soldiers, but only because good luck, for a change, was on their side. The two days following the battle, the sorrowing people did little more than drag themselves through the low grass-covered mountain passes. The wounded suffered from riding in the jolting travois, and several died. One was Ollokot's younger wife. A few of the very old and feeble ones begged to be left behind. Now their pleas were heard. Each was given a little food, a bowl of water, and a robe to keep them comfortable until they could "go home" to their mother, the earth. The only encouraging note for the people was the reports being brought in regularly by the rear guard that the Army was not pursuing them.

Not until the morning of August 13, did General Howard resume the chase. About noon, his soldiers reached the camp where the Nez Percés had left the old people.

The Bannock scouts who had been enlisted during the march across the Bitterroot Valley promptly killed and scalped the defenseless old ones. Then the Army moved on, having no difficulty following the wide swath left by the Nez Percés as they passed across the lush grass. By this time the Nez Percés were forty-five miles away to the southeast and picking up speed. They also were leaving death and destruction in their wake. The prime target was livestock. The chiefs were determined not to leave a horse or mule or cow for their pursuers to use. Settlers who objected to their taking the animals were killed. Near Birch Creek, they encountered a wagon train hauling supplies and liquor to a nearby settlement. A fight ensued in which the white men were killed and the merchandise stolen. The warriors guzzled the liquor, thereby becoming more violent than ever.

The settlers of southwestern Montana and adjoining Idaho "forted up" as best they could. Sixty Montanans organized a force and joined the troops. But first they addressed the general and criticized him strongly for not pressing a more vigorous pursuit. Then a delegation of angry Idahoans appeared and demanded he turn off the trail and protect their people. Being overly sensitive to criticism, he unwisely met these demands, and thus lost still another chance to overtake the Nez Percés, whom he now referred to as "Joseph's renegades." Meantime, the Nez Percés turned away from the Idaho settlements and made straight for Yellowstone National Park.

On August 19, General Howard finally resumed the chase and camped at Camas Meadows, a grassy place divided by two small streams. His troops raised their tents on an elevated lava knoll east of the creeks. Fifty-five volunteers from Montana's bustling gold camp of Virginia City reported in and established themselves in

*The Battle of Birch Creek,
from a sketch made on the field
during the fight.*

the middle of the broad meadow. Another fifty, all cavalrymen dispatched from Fort Ellis, settled down at the western edge.

Twenty-four hours earlier, the Nez Percés had camped here. One warrior had dreamed that his comrades went back over the trail and successfully stole the Army's horses. His dream, or vision, was discussed by the chiefs and a bold plan decided upon. After dark Ollokot, Toolhoolhoolzote, and Looking Glass led twenty-five warriors back to Camas Meadows. They stopped very close to the sleeping soldiers and picketed their horses.

Here are excerpts from Wottolen's account: "We divide into three companies. . . . Our company halts before drawing too near the enemy. The horses' feet must not be heard against the rocks. Active young men dismount and go forward among the enemy's horses, cutting them loose and removing bells from pack."

Peopeo Tholekt says the same, but adds: "I noticed a gray horse, a fine-looking horse, tied near this tent. I had my eyes on this horse. I went up to him, and I knew him. It was Chapman's horse, a swift runner. I was glad. I laughed to myself as I untied this gray horse. Just as I got it loose, one of our warriors fired his gun back in the rear. That alarmed the soldiers."

Wottolen continued: "Yelling loudly, the horses are quickly stampeded out from there. Back over trail they go, headed in right direction by Indians stationed for that business. . . . We do not stay to fight soldiers. We leave them firing like crazy people in the darkness. Nothing they can hit. We try driving the herd fast. Speed is slow. Daylight soon coming, we have only mules!"

The warriors were chagrined, yet their bold deed had deprived the Army of its pack string.

Later, Wottolen said: "Everybody knows it was Otskai who done the first shot. He did not obey orders of the leaders. We wanted to get close mixed with the soldiers. Everybody knew he did the carelessness. . . . Always Otskai was doing something like that. Crazy actions. Nervous, he broke our plans for getting the horses."

Otskai's shot started the horses nickering and brought soldiers from their tents. They did shoot in every direction and miraculously hit no one. The general bolted from his tent and roared for his trumpeter to rally the men. Soon order was restored, but more valuable time passed before three companies were dressed, armed and mounted, and ready to gallop off in pursuit. At this time the warriors, now eight miles away, were alerted by signals and knew the soldiers were coming. A few pushed on with the stolen herd, while the rest deployed themselves in a skirmish line across an open sagebrush flat.

Apparently the Indians didn't think much of what happened next, because as Wottolen said: "Long range shooting, nobody is hurt."

General Howard's report gave more details. On sighting the enemy, the companies deployed into left, center, and right positions in order to outflank the warriors' skirmish line. Norwood's company of cavalry got too far out in front and charged up a ridge of lava rock. They dropped back when they saw the Indians close at hand, dismounted, and sent their horses to the rear. Then they topped the ridge again and exchanged long shots with the enemy. The other companies ran into such hot resistance that they, too, dropped back to more secure positions. Seeing this, the warriors yowled triumphantly and advanced shooting. Many of the green troops fled, leaving Norwood's men badly exposed. They withdrew across open ground to a thicket of cottonwood and here fought valiantly and well. Those in complete rout ran head on into General Howard and more troops. He turned them around, and all raced to rescue Norwood. But the Indians saw them coming and beat a hasty retreat.

On reaching Norwood, the general halted. The Bannock scouts objected angrily and urged him to continue the pursuit. Instead, he turned back to Camas Meadows and spent another night there. By doing so he gave the Nez Percés time to cross over Targhee Pass and disappear into Yellowstone National Park.

On August 22, General Howard moved his force to beautiful Henry's Lake. Here his officers and the surgeons insisted on a three-day rest for the foot soldiers. After twenty-six days of marching, the soles of their cowhide shoes were worn through. In this mile-high country their thin blankets and summer uniforms provided scant protection against the chilly night temperatures. In addition, horses and fresh supplies were badly needed.

Accordingly, the general ordered the Virginia City volunteers to return to their gold camp and gather together the needed supplies and horses. He sent Norwood's men back to Fort Ellis to re-outfit and then proceed to the Crow reservation on the lower Yellowstone River, where the Nez Percés were expected to appear. Then the general and his staff rode to Virginia City, where a telegraph line would enable him to contact his superior officers.

His reception there was unpleasant. The volunteers had spared no words in condemning him publicly for "incompetence, blunders, and a failure to move fast enough." This information was reprinted in all regional newspapers and ultimately in San Francisco, Chicago, New York, and Washington, D.C. To add salt to his wounded pride, the

*Cyrenius Hall painted this
portrait of Chief Joseph in 1878.*

editors, who only a short time before had called the Nez Percés fiends and savages, now wrote glowingly of their prowess as warriors. Once again Joseph drew all the glory. He was described as "the splendid military intelligence that is leading their little handful of men, women and children, and possessions from one remote land to another, through an enemy's country and with five times their number of soldiers to intercept and pursue them."

These articles did much to turn public opinion against the Army and built sympathy for the Indians. Numerous individuals reminded the citizens of the many injustices committed against this tribe and their long attempt to live in peace. Small wonder that Joseph, and not General Howard, became the national hero of the hour.

In the report telegraphed to General Sherman on August 24, General Howard stated, among other reasons for a less than successful pursuit: "My command is so much worn by overfatigue and jaded animals that I cannot push it much further."

The supreme commander of the United States Army, perhaps overly sensitive to public criticism and angry because his over-all policy of extermination of the Indians was thwarted, despatched a stinging reply. He stated in part: ". . . that force of yours should pursue the Nez Percés to the death, lead where they may. . . . If you are tired, give the command to some young, energetic officer."

Deeply hurt by the inference that he was too old for the strenuous task, General Howard wired in answer: "You misunderstand me. I never flag. . . . You need not fear for the campaign. Neither you nor General McDowell can doubt my pluck and energy. . . . We move in the morning and will continue till the end."

XII The Escape
from Yellowstone National Park

The Nez Percés gained new heart from the daring theft of the Army mules. The chiefs had also guessed correctly that Howard must "sit down" until he replaced his pack animals. So, before crossing into Yellowstone National Park, the people tarried long enough to gather food. A nearby meadow abounded with fat grouse and elk, as well as their favorite bulbs and roots. A lake yielded hundreds of trout. When the Nez Percés finally got under way, their new, hastily woven food baskets were bulging with good things to eat. A long day's march brought them to the upper Madison River. Here another bounty of trout and elk was garnered before moving on into the Park.

Although Yellowstone National Park had been created by Congress, in 1872, at the urging of Montana citizens, the area was still in its original wild state. A poor wagon road had been hacked through the forest to make traveling easier for the several hundred tourists who came each year to view the awesome Grand Canyon of the Yellowstone River, the bubbling colored mud pools, and spouting geysers. This road, which was really only a trail, gave access to the various entrances leading from Montana, Idaho, and Wyoming into the park. The fleeing Nez Percés were familiar with portions of the region because an old Indian trail wound across the area north of the lake.

Since it was wiser to avoid contact with people, Poker Joe persuaded the chiefs to keep their route as secret as possible. To confuse their pursuers, they set forth on the Indian trail, but then doubled back to the river, crossed it, and cut through the timber. The going was rough, almost as bad as the Lolo Trail. But all remained in good spirits because the rear guard reported regularly that the soldiers were still "sitting down." Meanwhile, the advance scouts ranged far to the north and east and climbed the heights to spy on any other military columns which might be approaching.

On August 23, the families pitched camp in a beautiful meadow beside the Firehole River, the same river which the famed mountain man, Jim Bridger, claimed in his tall tales "ran cold on top and hot on the bottom." His statement was neither ridiculous nor a lie. The water tumbling down from distant snowbanks and mountainside springs was icy cold. But in places, warm springs bubbling up through the river bed did cause the river to run hot along the bottom. Since there were buffalo grazing here, the hunters killed several and distributed the meat among the families. The women dressed the hides as well as possible in the brief time available for this task. Their abrupt flight from the camps on the Clearwater and Big Hole had deprived the people of robes and clothing which had taken years to fashion. Since portions of the park were seven thousand feet high in elevation, even mid-August nights were chilly and early fall storms were common.

Some historians claim that had the Nez Percés abandoned their herd, they could have outdistanced the soldiers and escaped easily into Canada. Probably the size of the herd had been reduced by some five hundred animals at this point but moving the remainder of the herd through tangled country did slow the pace. But now that the families had lost so many possessions during their flight, they were loathe to lose their so-called "walking wealth." Also, having surplus ponies for the scouts and warriors to use already had proved valuable. Few of the mounts became so exhausted they had to be abandoned, while the Army pursuit was definitely hampered at crucial points in the future because its horses turned up lame.

From the Firehole River, Poker Joe led the way through a cat's cradle of steep timbered heights and deep ravines. This terrain still challenges the ablest of modern wilderness trekkers, who are never burdened with children, old folk, and excess baggage. Poker Joe was heading for the Absaroka Mountains, where thirty peaks, each over ten thousand feet high, formed the eastern Park boundary. The headwaters of two rivers spring forth on one peak in the extreme northeast sector. One is the Clark's Fork of the Yellowstone, named for the co-leader of the Lewis and Clark Expedition. It flows northward through a terrible canyon out onto the Crow reservation in Montana and then empties into the muddy lower Yellowstone River. The other is the Stinking Water (now called the Shoshone) which flows eastward through a slightly less rugged canyon of red rock and emerges from the mountains near present-day Cody, Wyoming. John Colter named it the Stinking Water in 1807 when he explored its canyon and discovered along its banks hot pools and fumaroles, or steam fissures, which emitted vaporous sulfuretted hydrogen that smelled like rotten eggs. Later this region became widely known as Colter's Hell.

While the families pressed toward these headwaters, one scouting party threaded its way straight north to the Mammoth Hot Springs area, or northern entrance to the park. Another ranged southward to the icy inland sea of Yellowstone Lake. Both encountered groups of two or three prospectors or tourists. The Indians murdered them to prevent their reaching General Howard with news of the Nez Percés' whereabouts.

A third party moved down the north-flowing Yellowstone River. They attacked the isolated ranchers who had settled along the foaming, green stream. They killed, looted and burned, and drove off the livestock. They made sure neither horses, nor cattle, nor foodstuffs nor wild game would be left within miles to help the troops when they finally came along. Finally they climbed to the bald summit of Cinnabar Mountain. Since they could see many miles of country in the crystal clear air, they spied two companies of cavalry approaching. The soldiers were accompanied by a wagon train of supplies and undoubtedly were being led by a large band of Crow scouts. The troops were expected, but the Crows were not. Now the warriors knew the worst. Their friends, the Crows, had become their enemies. After hurtling insults on the winds, the Nez Percé raiders hurried toward a small bridge which pioneer settlers had built across the river. They set fire to it and then galloped into the mountains.

About this time, August 27, General Howard resumed his pursuit with rested and re-outfitted troops. He was confident that capturing the non-Treaty Indians was only a matter of time. From a military viewpoint, Yellowstone National Park was a vast mountain fortress. However beautiful in summer, in winter the great depth of the snow which covered it and the extreme subzero cold rendered it unsuitable for any but the most rugged hunters. Even the elk fled the bitter winds of late October and sought the sunnier feeding grounds of the lower Yellowstone or Shoshone rivers. To linger too late in the fall when sudden blizzards closed the mountain passes was tantamount to suicide. So, as soon as his Bannock scouts, who knew the park, brought back word of the general direction the fleeing bands were taking, and the Treaty Nez Percé scouts assured him their relatives would move through Crow country to the Canadian border, the general laid elaborate plans to trap his quarry within the park.

His troops effectively blocked the northwest exit as an escape route. To close the other gateways, he appealed for help. General Sherman promptly ordered Lieutenant Gustavus C. Doane with two companies of cavalry and a party of Crow scouts to march from Fort Ellis to the Big Bend of the Yellowstone and on up the wild river toward Mammoth Hot Springs. This was the detachment which the renegades spied from atop Cinnabar Mountain. Next, General Sherman alerted the remnants of Custer's cavalry, torn to bits by the Sioux a year earlier. Numbering three hundred and sixty men, every one grimly set on revenge, they set forth under the command of Colonel Samuel D. Sturgis toward the mouth of the Clark's Fork of the Yellowstone, which is near present-day Billings, Montana. Their task was to block the northeast escape route. Then the General dispatched five more companies of cavalry under Major Hart to converge on Cody and block the eastern exit into Wyoming. Lastly, to cover the southeast pass through the Wind River Mountains, he moved out Colonel Wesley Merritt and ten companies of the Fifth Cavalry. When all outfits were on their way, the General relaxed. He had the Nez Percés so bottled up they could not possibly escape.

Once these troops took to the field, they relied on messengers to keep open lines of communication between General Sherman, various Montana forts, and General Howard. These vital duties were carried out by courageous men whose names and deeds gather dust in military archives. Alone or in pairs, they rode across miles of Indian-infested terrain. Some proved as adept at slipping unnoticed through the country as their Indian counterparts. At least a half dozen were killed in the line of duty.

Of course, General Sherman wasted no time in informing the nation of his plans to entrap the non-Treaty Nez Percés. He was surprised and angered to find that so much public sympathy had mushroomed in favor of the Indians. No doubt some of this was brought about by the many people who favored the underdog. But it was whetted by the accounts written by Thomas Sutherland and other newspaper reporters who joined General Howard's troops from time to time. Their stories of how the Nez Percés were outfighting and outmaneuvering the sol-

When public sympathy for the Nez Percé was at its height, this drawing was published with the following caption written under it: "Me no want to kill a man who can't shoot."

diers made exciting reading and put the Army in a bad light. Some of the sympathy directed toward the Nez Percés was deserved, but some of it was also badly misplaced. There was no denying the fact that a good many of the warriors, starting with the raids on the Idaho settlements, were guilty of vandalism, robbery, and coldblooded murder. For them to fight in self-defense was admirable, but to rampage and kill was criminal.

Some of the correspondents and acid-penned editors pictured General Howard and his troops as little more than bumbling incompetents. Admittedly, the General left much to be desired as a commander. Nevertheless his troops performed well against the dual enemy of wilderness and Indians. The average reader simply could not comprehend the hardships of a mountain-country campaign. Here the Nez Percés had a decided advantage over their foe. They were long-used to moving through country that, in places, seemed to stand on end. They did not need a corps of axemen to clear the way. They knew how to live off the land. Their ponies remained strong, feeding on the native grass, and they had enough horses so that when one mount grew tired, there was a fresh one to replace it.

In contrast, the troops were tied to slow, cumbersome pack trains for supplies. When their horses and uniforms gave out, they had to wait for replacements. Army horses and mules quickly grew gaunt without their daily ration of oats. Many labored on until they dropped from exhaustion. Thus at times when General Howard appeared to be dawdling, his delays were unavoidable. Yet the records show only too plainly that he muffed numerous advantages, any one of which would have brought the war to a mercifully quick conclusion.

By September 5, the troops had crossed the park and reached the pleasant open valley of the Lamar River. A major tributary of the Yellowstone, this stream also flowed down from the heights where the Clark's Fork and Stinking Water bubbled forth. Its valley was well-known to Indian and white trappers and prospectors. While he was camped here, the General received exciting news. His scouts learned definitely that the Nez Percés were approaching the headwaters in the Absaroka Mountains. Then messengers arrived with word that troops were waiting at the mouth of the Clark's Fork, and others at the Stinking Water. At last, the Indians were trapped between two strong military forces. Since escape was impossible, he jubilantly despatched a messenger to Fort Ellis with word that the capture now was only days away.

This information was relayed by telegraph to General Sherman and the regional newspapers. *The New Northwest,* published in Montana, stated: "We wait now hopefully for news that the Nez Percés have been struck hard and fatally. They are too brave and too dangerous a foe to escape, for their escape unscathed means still darker days for the border."

Unfortunately, the news that Colonel Sturgis and his troops were laying in wait at the mouth of the Clark's Fork was no longer accurate by the time it reached Howard's ears. The colonel had arrived by September 2, and gone into camp. He waited for news of General Howard's whereabouts, but none was forthcoming because Howard's messengers were killed on their way out of the Park. Sturgis began to fret and worry. Part of his concern was based on the fact that his son had died the summer before in the Custer massacre. Hatred smouldered in his heart for all Indians, whether or not they had anything to do with his son's death. Also, those of his men who had been part of Custer's companies, fighting apart from those overwhelmed by the Sioux, now ached to revive the Seventh Cavalry's former reputation as the finest Indian fighters in the West. Thus, when Colonel Sturgis' scouts reported no sign of Nez Percés coming their way, he feared they had turned instead toward the Stinking Water.

On September 7, a prospector came down out of the mountains and stated positively he had seen the Nez Percés heading east. Now alarmed, Sturgis doublemarched his men around the east slope of the mountains toward the Stinking Water. They did not encounter Major Hart's force because it had not yet reached the critical area. At the river, the colonel warned his men that an enemy attack might occur at any moment. They moved upriver in an advance which was a model of taut-nerved readiness. On September 10, they attained the heights without mishap, only to learn their prey had escaped!

Thanks to the superb reconnoitering of the Nez Percé scouts, Poker Joe and the chiefs knew all about General Howard's advance to the Lamar Valley. They had seen Lieutenant Doane's men approaching. With field glasses, they picked out Colonel Sturgis' camp at the mouth of Clark's Fork. Most important, they reported swiftly when this force pulled away and headed east around the mountains. Poker Joe cheered on learning this and planned an escape route. He knew the canyon of the Clark's Fork was passable. It was a nightmare—gloomy, formidable and far worse than the Lolo Trail—but it was passable. The chiefs readily agreed to tackle it.

First the people moved out on the trail leading toward the Stinking Water. This was the movement observed by General Howard's scouts and by the prospector who had reported to Colonel Sturgis. But these spies left the scene too soon. The Nez Percés continued eastward at a purposely leisurely pace and even paused for a long rest. As soon as their scouts reported that the Army scouts had withdrawn, the camp buzzed with activity. The men and women milled the horses and mules round and round over a large area until the trail was thoroughly confused. Then, avoiding the trail, they doubled back silently through the forest. Their passage through this tangled country now ranks as one of the most superb feats of its kind in western history. Poker Joe led the way to the brink of the dark narrow canyon and picked his way down the dark and very dangerous slope. In places the rocks came so close together that everyone, afoot or on horseback, had difficulty squeezing through. Many a pack was rubbed off a mule's back.

The last of the Indian column had barely disappeared into the shadowy depths when General Howard's scouts returned to the scene. They rode within rifle shot of the last of the Nez Percés without seeing them and continued on down the trail leading to the Stinking Water. When they came to the place where the Nez Percé ponies had milled about, it took them over two hours to solve the riddle. Furious at being outwitted, they whipped their ponies in a fast race back to General Howard. By this time it was late afternoon. Since an ambush in the canyon was all too possible, he chose to lay over until very early the next morning. He was not unduly worried because he still thought Colonel Sturgis was posted at the mouth of the canyon.

Meanwhile, the Nez Percés pressed on by starlight. At daybreak they emerged from the canyon. With no troops to hold them, they ran free and clear to a long-used fording on the Yellowstone River.

"THE NEZ PERCÉS' STATE CARRIAGE."

A group of Nez Percé warriors
make off with a stagecoach
near the Yellowstone.

XIII   The Skirmish at Canyon Creek

Not until the Nez Percés crossed the Yellowstone River did a sigh of relief sweep the length of the column. Their whoops of joy rent the air. They had outwitted the Army and the hated Bannock scouts. Now the buffalo range was at hand. Traveling on the vast sun-cured sweep of grassland in good weather was pure joy. After a brief rest, the march was resumed with everyone in good spirits. The brilliant sunlight was as comforting as a soft robe.

The peace they sought loomed close, almost in sight on the northernmost edge of the golden prairie. No more monstrous rivers or bleak mountains would tax their weary bodies. Instead of sighing and groaning, the women began to chatter lightheartedly. The children's laughter blended with the sweet piping of flocks of prairie larks. As the ponies discovered the softer ground was a balm to their rock-bruised hooves, they nickered and even frolicked a little.

Yet the grim business of war could not be forgotten for long. There were enemies near, white ranchers and prospectors who were dangeous. Since the Nez Percés had no means of handling prisoners and dared not run the risk of having these unfortunates act as messengers for the military outfits to the rear, the warriors killed them. The victims' food, clothing, utensils, weapons, and cartridges —all were taken to replace the articles lost at the Big Hole.

One large party of warriors sighted a ranch in the distance. It was a regular stage station stopover on the run from Bismarck, in the Dakota Territory, through the Yellowstone Valley and on to Bozeman, near Fort Ellis. A stagecoach was just then unloading at the ranch. Three passengers stepped down, glad to have some relief from the bruising ride. One was young and pretty Fanny Clark, a very popular vaudeville performer who was touring the Montana settlements. Before she could shake the dust from her traveling suit, the ranch owner, Bill Brockway, spied dust rising in the distance and made out the figures of horses. He shouted, "Injuns coming! Take cover!"

All raced for a willow thicket nearby. Not long afterward, the warriors rushed on the scene. The stagecoach horses were spooked by the Indian smell and prepared to run. But one warrior leaped on the back of a lead horse and controlled them skillfully. The others swarmed over the coach, ripped open the trunks, and draped the actress' costumes and fancy hats on themselves. Then they tore the mail sacks to pieces. Next they plundered and set fire to the ranch buildings. Then they returned to the coach, tied their ponies to the rear, climbed aboard, and dashed away, whooping excitedly.

At least no one was harmed in this raid. But others died as the Nez Percés continued their policy of clearing enemies, horses, and wild game from their path. About this same time, some of the women began protesting that the pace was too fast. They thought that since the enemy was far behind, there was no need to hurry. Poker Joe argued strongly for a forced march that would continue until all were safely across the Canadian border. Looking Glass saw a chance to make trouble for the half-breed who had succeeded him as leader. In his forceful way, he insisted the people were weakening from the strain of the prolonged flight and must rest. Angry words were exchanged as the chiefs took sides, but Poker Joe had his way. The march resumed, and none too soon. Very soon word came from the rear guard that the soldiers had crossed the Yellowstone River.

Days before, Colonel Sturgis and his men had followed General Howard's slow trek down the canyon of the Clark's Fork and caught up with them when they made camp at the mouth of the canyon. The two leaders faced the glum fact that once more a heavily burdened pack of savages had outwitted them. With great reluctance, the general despatched the disappointing news on to his superior officers. He could almost feel the withering blast of scorn that would be directed toward him now.

Colonel Sturgis was very anxious to make up for his blunder, and his men were chafing for action. So the general transferred his two mountain howitzers and fifty of his ablest marksmen to the colonel's command. He ordered Sturgis to carry on the chase, overtake the enemy, and hold them until he could arrive to finish them off. Even if Sturgis could whip the varmints, he was not to do so. He was to let the general move in for the final kill.

After a rousing send-off of cheers and gunfire, the colonel and four hundred men pressed hard toward the Yellowstone River. They traveled sixty miles in one day and sloshed across the river. After a brief rest, they continued northward. Not long afterward, they were joined by several Crow scouts, who claimed they had sighted the main body of Nez Percés only six miles to the north. Within moments the soldiers were galloping across the open ground, their company guidons snapping in the wind. The dust they raised was seen by the Nez Percé rear guard, who flashed a warning to the people.

"Soldiers coming!" the chiefs shouted to the families who were strung out in a long column. Immediately those guarding the horse herd shrieked until the animals broke into a run. The women hurried their pack train up the dry stream bed of Canyon Creek. They sought the canyon, which was little more than a narrow boulder-strewn valley enclosed on both sides with steep rimrock. Meantime, some of the warriors, led by Looking Glass, formed a line across the mouth of the canyon. The younger men, led by Ollokot, scrambled to the top of the rimrock, found vantage points behind boulders, and waited for the soldiers to come within range. As soon as Joseph and White Bird saw the last family enter the canyon, they ordered the younger women and boys to pause at various spots and raise barriers of rock and brush. Then Joseph hastened to the front, urging everyone to "hurry, hurry" and never flag for one moment.

As soon as the Nez Percés were sighted, Colonel Sturgis gave the order to charge. His troops raced ahead until those in front began toppling in the face of Nez Percé gunfire. His next command proved to be a grievous tactical error. He ordered his forward company to dismount, string out in a skirmish line, and advance on foot. This ruined his chance to overwhelm the enemy. Some of his men actually wept with rage when they were forced to inch forward with only clumps of sagebrush for cover. A second mounted company tried twice to storm the rimrock. The Indian sharpshooters drove them back.

Yellow Wolf said later: "We did not line up like soldiers. We went by ones, just here and there entering the canyon."

Unlike Custer, who always charged at the front with his best marksmen, the colonel stationed himself a half mile to the rear. He watched the action through field glasses. When he saw the families pulling away up the canyon, he ordered the big guns fired. These shots fell short. Then he made another blunder. When a young officer rode back and pleaded for permission to charge the canyon, Sturgis refused. He was afraid that a face-to-face fight would develop. The fact that it did not was due to the warriors' intention not to engage in fighting at close quarters. They put forth a strong delaying action until

The Battle of Canyon Creek.

the families escaped from the canyon. Then they leaped on their ponies and disappeared. Thanks to the sharpshooters atop the rim, they were able to escape unharmed.

At sunset the colonel gave up the fight. Weary and angry, the troopers dragged back to his position. Immediately, quarreling broke out between the colonel and his officers about who was to blame for the outcome. Again the Nez Percés had squeaked past disaster. The military could do no more than lick its wounds and wait for supplies and reinforcements to arrive. Meanwhile the Nez Percés rushed on until midnight and put fifteen miles between themselves and the soldiers. Then, after a few hours' rest in a cottonwood grove, they pressed on.

The next morning, September 14, General Howard rode into Sturgis' camp with an additional fifty cavalrymen. The remainder of his force and the supply train

were far to the rear. He was dismayed to learn what had happened. The colonel reported three men had been killed, eleven wounded, and nearly fifty horses shot. But he assured Howard the Indians had suffered greatly and had abandoned nine hundred ponies. This was far from the truth. The Nez Percés lost no warriors, had three wounded slightly, and abandoned only forty of their poorest mounts.

However, at about this time, trouble swept over them from an unexpected source. Two hundred of the Army's Bannock and Crow scouts had slipped out on their own in search of Nez Percé scalps. By riding hard they caught up with the rear guard and began shooting. As Yellow Wolf described the action, they came up fast "hanging low on the sides of their horses, doing under-neck shooting. . . . Only when we were moving would they come after us. When we met them, they ran from us." His description is not exactly correct. All that day the Nez Percé warriors were forced to defend the rear and flanks of their column. The next morning they repulsed a charge with great difficulty. Only then did the frustrated Crows and Bannocks give up the fight and retreat.

This was the last attack for a few days. During the brief respite from harassment, the people forded the shallow Musselshell River and hurried toward the Missouri River. They reached it by midday of September 23, having covered seventy-five miles in thirty-six hours. The families dropped, exhausted, on the grass. But the warriors began pointing across the river and shouting excitedly. In plain view was a great mound of bales and boxes, and obviously less than a dozen men standing guard.

Unknowingly the Nez Percés had come to the river at the point, marked by an island, which was the head of navigation. Steamboats transporting soldiers, settlers, and supplies from St. Louis and Fort Leavenworth could go no further. They unloaded at this point on the north bank of the river. The goods were transferred to ox-drawn freight wagons for shipment on to various Montana forts and settlements. Often days elapsed between the unloading and pickup, and this is why the goods were still stacked on the bank.

Four civilians and twelve troopers had been left to guard the shipment. As soon as they spied the Nez Percés, they began digging a rifle pit behind a large stack of packing cases. It was barely finished when twenty warriors led by Looking Glass and Ollokot crossed the river and, with a few shots, pinned down the guards. Joseph led the main column across and pushed on two miles before telling the people they might sit down. Immediately most of the warriors raced back to the river. Here they joined the others in carrying off as many crates and boxes as possible. The looting continued all night.

Peopeo Tholekt said later: "We took whatever we needed. . . . Some took pans and pots for cooking. We figured it was soldier supplies, so set fire to what we did not take. We had privilege to do this. It was war."

The rich haul included sacks of flour, sugar (which the Indians prized), rice, and beans. Just before daylight the warriors lifted their siege and returned to camp. By this time Joseph had everyone ready to travel. Poker Joe said there was an easy pass between the Little Rockies and the Bear Paw Mountains which lay between them and Canada. On hearing this, some of the families pleaded they were too tired to go on. But Joseph coaxed until they agreed to move. By noon they and many more were complaining loudly of fatigue. Again Joseph exerted himself with cajoling until all stumbled to their feet and resumed the journey. However, in the late afternoon a good many sat down and refused to budge. This time even Joseph argued for a rest when Poker Joe tried to force an all-night march on the people.

The chiefs and warriors gathered in a council while the women struggled to set up camp. Admittedly nerves were raw from the strain of the long flight, and tempers were frayed from fatigue. Yellow Wolf reminded Poker Joe that Cut-Arm's shooters were two days behind, so the people were safe. They should be allowed to rest. Then Looking Glass shook his fist at the hunter and upbraided him for hurrying and causing the old people weariness.

Sarcastically, he reminded Poker Joe that he was no chief. He, Looking Glass, was the chief now. He was taking over as leader.

Poker Joe looked each of the chiefs squarely in the face. He reminded them that he had brought them through to this point so close to Canada and safety. He warned that it was very bad to slow down now. If the people would only keep going another twenty-four or forty-eight hours, the soldiers could not touch one child, one pony.

But the chiefs would not listen. Their wives and relatives had told them they would not move until they had had some rest.

Finally, Poker Joe said, "All right, Looking Glass, you can lead. I am trying to save the people, doing my best to cross into Canada before the soldiers find us. You can take command. But I think we will be caught and killed."

In spite of the fact that Looking Glass's decision earlier to let the people dawdle had brought them to disaster in the Big Hole Valley, and that he had been rejected as their war leader, the chiefs once more put the lives of their people in the hands of Looking Glass.

XIV The Battle
at the Bear Paw Mountains

Since hours of daylight remained, the warriors went hunting. There were no trees within miles, so the women and children pried dried cakes of buffalo dung from the grass and used these as a substitute for firewood. Not long afterward, the hunters began straggling in with great haunches of buffalo meat. These were cut up and set to cooking. Meantime, the goods stolen from the supply depot were distributed to the families. They whooped joyfully over boxes of Army-issue underdrawers and boots. The children bent double laughing as their fathers donned the boots and clumped about, mocking the soldiers. The women exclaimed excitedly over the shiny new kettles and ripped open the sacks of coffee beans and rice. But the biggest treat was the sugar. As each sack was dumped on the ground, the people jostled each other good-naturedly to get at them. Some scooped up the sugar by the handful and crammed their mouths full. Others wet their hands first, coated them, and then stood about, grinning as they licked their fingers clean. *Ayee!* It was good to have time to laugh and relax.

Only among the Wallowa band was a sadness noted. Joseph's people instinctively disliked the open plain. They mistrusted it, and felt exposed, almost naked. They wrinkled their noses at the sour smoke rising from the buffalo chips and yearned for the clean-smelling aroma of burning pine and spruce. Some of the old ones wept and clung to Joseph. He comforted them, promising that very soon they would camp in a grassy draw with the timbered Bear Paw Mountains to the west and the Little Rocky Mountains to the east. These were low, isolated spurs of the soaring continental divide, farther west, their timbered flanks seemingly afloat in an ocean of grass. And only one day's march beyond them, Joseph added, the good people would cross over into Canada. There the strong-hearted Sioux people would welcome them. "No soldiers there," he said over and over until the old ones brushed away their tears.

The next morning, Looking Glass gave the people all the time they wanted for a leisurely breakfast. They were late in getting underway and put few miles behind them before the women began clamoring for an early halt. Looking Glass obliged them then and for the following three days. Since the scouts ranging far to the south reported no sign of approaching soldiers, he felt confident there was no danger. Thus, feeling more secure than they had in weeks, the people entered the valley which separated the two small ranges of mountains. On the morning of September 29, they passed beyond the northernmost slope of the Little Rockies. Now to their right, the country opened out into rolling grassland, but the Bear Paw Mountains still loomed up ten miles away on their left.

During that morning, the long spell of good weather came to an end. A cold wind from the north brought low scudding clouds which blotted out the sun. The temperature quickly chilled. Since so many robes and extra clothing had been lost during the battle in the Big Hole, there were not sufficient coverings to protect them from the increasing cold. About midday, the people came in sight of a narrow twisting stream which meandered below the level of the valley floor. The low banks were cut with brush-choked coulees between five and ten feet deep. A great clamor rose the length of the column as the women urged Looking Glass to seek shelter from the wind. They feared a storm was approaching, and it would be very bad to be caught out on the exposed plain.

Looking Glass agreed only to seek the shelter of the coulees for a midday rest period. The column turned toward the creek, the people scurrying down the bluff to claim camping spots in the coulees. While the women started their cookfires, the chiefs and leading warriors gathered as usual for a council. A brave fighter named Wottolen asked permission to speak. He said he had had a bad dream the night before in which he saw soldiers rushing down over the people and killing many of them. He urged Looking Glass to "hurry, hurry up" and not stop until everyone was safe in Canada.

Normally the chiefs would have given Wottolen's

dream careful consideration and probably acted upon it, because they put great store in dreams. But Looking Glass gave them no opportunity for discussion. He laughed in Wottolen's face and called him a coward. He reminded all those present that Cut-Arm was a safe two day's march from the people. Therefore, he was not going to expose the people to the danger of being caught out on the shelterless plain in the face of an oncoming storm. He would let them wait it out in this snug camp.

Only then did an argument flare. White Bird reminded Looking Glass that when Wahlitits had a bad dream the night before the people sat down beside the Big Hole River, the war chief had ignored the portent of his dream. The result had been a terrible disaster. Now Looking Glass must not ignore the spirit message in Wottolen's dream. He must keep the people moving, or else Wottolen's dream would come true. But the warriors sided with Looking Glass because their families were already suffering from the cold. Besides, a storm that would delay their people would also stall the soldiers. This was so obviously true that all present agreed to wait out this first storm of the season within the shelter of the bluffs.

After the council disbanded, the chiefs returned to their separate bands. In a north-to-south line along the stream which was named Snake Creek, first camped Toolhoolhoolzote and the few survivors of his little band. Separated from them in the adjoining coulees were White Bird's people, and next to them, Looking Glass's camp. Joseph and the Wallowas sat down at the southernmost end, Poker Joe sharing Joseph's hospitality. Less than three hundred yards from his camp, a high ridge blocked the view to the south. According to the records, he and Poker Joe

An Army officer drew these portraits of three of the leading Army officers in the Nez Percé war: General Oliver O. Howard, Colonel (later General) Samuel D. Sturgis, and General Nelson A. Miles.

climbed the ridge several times between midday and dark to look for some sign of soldiers approaching. But since they saw nothing alarming, and the scouts out there flashed no warning, they returned to the shelter the women had fashioned from mats and tangled brush. Again the hunters brought in a great quantity of buffalo meat so fires blazed brightly all along the creek. Not long after dark it began to snow, and the cold sharpened. The families retired early, the adults sleeping with the children between them to give them added warmth. The ponies turned tail to the storm, and at long last the scouts rode in to snatch a few hour's sleep.

Actually, the exiles were safe for the time being from the combined forces of Colonel Sturgis and General Howard. These troops were advancing at a very slow pace, but deliberately so, in order to fool the Nez Percés. A new trap had been set for them, and Howard wanted them to become overconfident. Meantime a large outfit, well-mounted and strong, had assembled at Fort Keogh, which was located at the confluence of the Tongue River and the lower Yellowstone. This included 383 cavalrymen and mounted infantrymen and thirty Cheyenne Indian scouts under the command of Colonel Nelson A. Miles. His orders were to move northwestward across the buffalo plain, but to stay east of the Little Rockies. When his scouts saw the Nez Percés merge from the valley between those mountains and the Bear Paws, he was to run them down.

Since the Nez Percés did slow up and made no effort to conceal their presence on the plain, the Cheyenne scouts had no difficulty spying on their progress and reporting back to Colonel Miles. On September 29, when the families went into camp along Snake Creek, the soldiers came on as quietly and cautiously as possible. The Little Rockies shielded them from being seen by those in camp. The blustering wind dissipated their dust so the scouts could not see them approaching. Besides, the scouts were looking only to the south for a sign of Cut-Arm's advance. On the night of September 29, Miles' force camped out on the plain without raising tents or lighting fires. About four A.M., the men were roused, not by trumpeters, but by the night guards moving quietly from group to group. After munching a little hardtack, they saddled up and formed ranks in the column. Hand signals were used to get the column in motion.

The Nez Percés had also wakened early. By six A.M., the cookfires were blazing, and many of the people were eating. A few had finished and brought their ponies from the herd in order to fasten the packs. At this time, two of the hunters who had camped out on the plain all night rode hurriedly into camp. They said they had seen buffalo running east of the Little Rockies. Since this could mean that the animals were running from soldiers, some of the families took fright. They ran for their ponies. But Looking Glass called to them not to panic. "Plenty, plenty time," he shouted. "Let the children eat all wanted."

A few ignored his suggestion and packed their horses. But mostly, the women told the children to go on eating or playing. An hour passed, and then a scout atop the ridge south of the camp flapped his blanket. Those who saw it shouted excitedly, "Soldiers coming!"

A warrior named Shot in Head told this story: "Everybody was outside, running here, there, everywhere. . . . . Horses running in every direction. Women, old men and

General Miles' troops charge the Indian camp.

young men trying to capture saddle horses. The trying was vain. I ran to one I saw staked out and jumped to his back. I went to the camp for my gun. . . . I rode to another part of the camp where I found two other warriors, and we all started over the hill to face the soldiers. We went up, one by one, the passing bullets singing close to us. . . . Then down the outside of the line we went, bullets buzzing like summer flies."

Black Eagle said: "I heard a rumbling like stampeding buffalos to the south and looking I saw troops galloping toward us. I knew well what that meant, and I ran for the horses. I had soldier shoes on which were too large and heavy for the swift going. I stopped and took them off, leaving them there on the ground."

White Bird's young nephew added: "It was morning and we children were playing. We had hardwood sticks, throwing mud balls. I looked up and saw a spotted horse, a Cheyenne warrior, wearing a war bonnet, come to the bluff above me. He was close followed by some troops. Some of the children ran back to the camps. Some hurried to the gulch."

Another boy said later: "My father told me to run out from there, to skip for my life. We ran for our horses. Shooting began, and our horses became stampeded. Everybody caught whatever horse they could. . . . I ran my horse about a half mile when I thought of my little brother that I had left. I find him, and getting him up behind me, we go. . . . I got away from that war alive. . . . How I escaped was, I was not completely surrounded."

From that first shouted warning, the Nez Percé camp was the scene of utter confusion. Some of the chiefs and warriors grabbed their weapons and raced to the ridge. Those families who were already packed fled northward. Joseph and his helpers raced toward the horses. Their first responsibility was to bring back enough so the women and children could escape more swiftly than if they ran. But before Joseph could reach the herd, the soldiers started shooting. The shots spooked the animals. They reared back, snorted, and ran away.

The soldiers closed in fast. A solid line of one hundred and fifteen men and mounts pounded toward the ridge. With incredible coolness, the warriors held their fire until the soldiers almost overran them. Then they unleashed a deadly volley. All along the line, troopers toppled to the ground. Their horses screamed and milled around. A second volley sent more soldiers pitching out of their saddles. The line shattered, and the wild charge broke as the survivors raced to the rear, leaving the dead and wounded behind.

While the front line was charging, another swung around and raced down on the camp from the west. These soldiers bowled into the herd, scattering the ponies, and then fought the Indians at close quarters. Joseph had just caught a pony. He boosted his eldest daughter on its back and told her to ride north. Then he made his way across to his camp. Here is how he described his plight: "I thought of my wife and children, who were now surrounded by soldiers, and I resolved to go to them or die. With a prayer in my mouth to the Great Spirit Chief who rules above, I dashed unarmed through the line of soldiers. It seemed to me there were guns on every side, before and behind me. My clothes were cut to pieces and my horse was wounded, but I was not hurt. As I reached the door of my lodge, my wife handed me my rifle, saying, 'Here's your gun. Fight!'

"The soldiers kept up a continuous fire. Six of my men were killed in one spot near me. Ten or twelve soldiers charged into our camp and got possession of two lodges, killing three Nez Percés and losing three of their men who fell inside our lines. I called my men to drive them back. We fought at close range, not more than twenty steps apart and drove the soldiers back upon their main line, leaving their dead in our hands. We secured their arms and ammunition."

The first charge cost the Army fifty-three men killed or wounded. One cavalry troop lost sixty per cent of its members. As the survivors of this frontal attack took flight, Colonel Miles and a detachment of the Fifth Cavalry arrived. He ordered a second charge, and the trumpeter sounded the summons. Every man swung into a new line and charged forward. Again the Nez Percés raked them with gunfire. Some of the soldiers dismounted and fired from kneeling or prone positions. When this proved too costly, they mounted again and drew back. Meantime an artillery squad swung wide to the west, raced to a position north of the village, and attempted to lob shots from the howitzer down on the camp. Sharpshooters killed every one.

Now Colonel Miles ordered his troops to surround the camp, dig pits with their bayonets, and exchange shot for shot with the exiles. While this was being effected, he surveyed his situation. It was not encouraging. Even before he had left Fort Keogh, his Cheyenne scouts had told him that Sitting Bull and two thousand Sioux were camped just beyond the Canadian border. If Joseph got word to them, and very likely messengers already were on their way, Sitting Bull might sweep down and rescue the Nez Percés. Thus it was imperative that the soldiers whip them before nightfall. So as soon as the companies were reformed and the horses under control, he ordered three companies to sweep around the ridge and hit the camp from the southwest. He hoped this would drive the Indians across the creek and out on the plain, away from their shelters and supply of water.

Again the warriors were too much for the troops. Though one squad did manage to storm a high point and kill a number of warriors, many clung to their rifle pits.

By nightfall the Nez Percés were far from defeated. During this time the supply train had caught up with Colonel Miles. He ordered tents raised, fires built, and a hot meal prepared for his men. One by one they pulled back to the rear.

After the soldiers' firing ceased, the warriors left their posts. All were anxious to see how their families had fared. Each chief took a nose count. Alahoos, an old man, was the people's crier. He moved from campfire to campfire, and the chiefs told him who was missing, or wounded, or dead. He carried the news from one band to another until all the people knew what had happened that day. Soon shrieks rent the air as Toolhoolhoolzote's death became known. Then White Bird and Looking Glass each counted several warriors and women killed. But even in their grief all mourned with Joseph when he said that Poker Joe and Joseph's brother Ollokot had been killed on the heights that day.

Yellow Wolf spoke for all when he described later how his people felt when they counted twenty-two dead. He said: "I felt the end coming. All for which we had suffered [was] lost! Thoughts came of the Wallowa where I grew up. Of my own country when only Indians were there. Of tepees along the bending river. Of the blue clear lake, wide meadows with horse and cattle herds. From the mountain forests, voices seemed calling [me]. I felt as dreaming. Not my living self. . . . Then with rifle I stood forth, saying to my heart, 'Here I will die, fighting for my people and our homes!' "

XV   Surrender

While the women and children wailed, Looking Glass bade his crier summon the few remaining chiefs and their warriors to a council. After all had sat down around the fire, the war leader declared that he meant to fight until every man, woman, and child was dead. Most accepted his decision, though some murmured they preferred to bolt for freedom through the soldiers' line. But this was only talk. Nearly all the ponies were gone now, and in such a foolish action the women and children would be the first to die. Six young warriors, sick at heart now that Ollokot was dead, volunteered to crawl on their stomachs past the soldiers and go on foot through the darkness and storm to appeal to Sitting Bull for help. After a tearful farewell with their families they slipped away, never to be heard from again.

Next the bodies of the dead were prepared for burial: the faces painted, the spirit tokens placed in the hands, dried roots and pinches of dirt sprinkled on the chests, the remains sewed in robes. After that came the task of digging shallow holes in the sides of the coulees so the dead could rest in secret places where the Cheyenne scouts could not find them and desecrate the graves. Once this sorrowful duty was done, every able person, even the old ones who could scarcely hold a buffalo horn in their trembling hands, commenced digging. They deepened the natural shelters of the coulees, opened jug-shaped pits and connected some with small tunnels.

One of the women said later: "We digged the trenches with camas hooks and butcher knives. With pans we threw out the dirt. We could not do much cooking. Dried meat and some other grub would be handed around. If not enough for all, it would be given the children first. . . . Children cried with hunger and cold. Old people suffered in silence. Misery everywhere."

When it was time for the warriors to return to the defensive positions, they embraced their families. Then gathering up their weapons, food, and robes, they climbed out of the creek bottom. As they scuttled across the grass and picked their way to the heights, the wind pummeled them. Their moccasins sank in five inches of snow. Bending low, they spread out along the ridge top or hid themselves behind boulders or barricades of loose rock. As always, some fighters remained with or close to the families to protect them. By daylight all were ready for the battle to begin again.

The soldiers opened the attack by firing cannon shot along the creek. The Nez Percés suffered no casualties

*While the warriors fought, the Nez Percé women
sought refuge in trenches they had dug.*

until a direct hit caved in a shelter, burying a woman and
her child. Meantime the storm continued, making things
difficult for the sharpshooters on both sides. Toward
noon, Colonel Miles realized that a stalemate existed.
This kind of fight could go on for days. He wanted action
now and for two widely different reasons. First, every
hour he expected to see a strong force of Sioux ride in
to the rescue and wipe out his men just as they had massacred Custer the year before. And second, he wanted the
glory of subduing the Nez Percés for himself and his soldiers. But somewhere off to the south General Howard
was approaching with his troops. When he arrived, he
would assume command, finish off the Indians, and re-
store his tarnished image with a bright victory.

After much thought, the course of action which Miles decided upon surprised both his men and the Indians. When the storm slackened, he made the first venture toward getting Joseph to surrender. He had a white flag run up. When Joseph did not appear, he ordered an interpreter to approach the enemy line with the flag and sing out, "Miles would like to see Joseph."

From this crucial moment on, eyewitness accounts gained from Indians and the military disagree on a number of points. But apparently on seeing the white flag, Looking Glass, White Bird, and Joseph talked together. The first two refused to answer the summons. Looking Glass was positive the flag was a trick. He reminded Joseph that the white chiefs could not be trusted in any way. Then both he and White Bird made it clear they would never surrender.

Joseph answered that because the families were suffering from the cold, he would listen to what Miles had to say. So, with two warriors at his side, he walked out toward a point where a buffalo robe had been laid on the snow. Colonel Miles and several of his staff joined them there.

The Army interpreter made the introductions and told Joseph that Colonel Miles was a humane and honorable man. After some talk, the colonel asked Joseph to surrender. Joseph refused, but added that his people wanted only to return peaceably to their homeland. Miles pointed out that the Nez Percés were in a desperate situation. General Howard and Colonel Sturgis and all their troops would arrive soon. It would be better to surrender all the guns now. If this were done, the colonel either promised, or suggested, he would take the Nez Percés to Fort Keogh and see them comfortably encamped beside the Tongue River. In the spring, he would escort them back to the Nez Percé reservation.

Joseph thought this proposal was good because the Wallowas had never ceased clamoring to go home. But he said the people could not surrender all their guns because they needed some for hunting. The two haggled over this point until Joseph rose to leave. Some witnesses say he left to talk with Looking Glass and White Bird and that Lieutenant Lovell H. Jerome accompanied him. Others claim the lieutenant walked to the camp with Joseph's comrades to make sure the Nez Percés did surrender their guns while Joseph accepted Miles's invitation to come to his tent for more talk and a cup of coffee. One way or another, Joseph followed Miles, feeling secure because the truce flag still fluttered in the wind. But the moment he stepped inside the tent, he was taken prisoner. His hands and feet were bound, and he was hustled along to the place where the pack mules were picketed. He was pushed to the ground, a buffalo robe thrown over him, and left out all night.

The Nez Percés waited for him to return. When it was obvious he had been captured, Lieutenant Jerome found himself surrounded with menacing warriors who threatened to tear him to pieces. But Looking Glass shouted them down and placed the prisoner in custody of Wottolen and Yellow Bull. He was not disarmed, nor bound, and was marched to a dugout where he was given food, water, and a robe.

Looking Glass told the people about this newest instance of white treachery and bade them prepare for another battle on the morrow. Throughout the night they

A contemporary drawing shows Lieutenant Jerome bei waited on by Nez Percé wom while being held as hostage.

deepened the shelters and rifle pits, all the while suffering in the dark, damp, cold holes. As Ollokot's wife said: "We slept only by naps, sitting in our pits, leaning forward or back against the dirt wall." In contrast, the soldiers enjoyed the modest comforts of campfires, hot food, and tents.

The shooting resumed at daybreak of the third day. But there were long pauses between the outbursts because the Nez Percés dared not waste a single shot. Midmorning one of the warriors on the ridge signaled that riders were approaching fast from the north. As the good news was shouted throughout the camp, the people cheered. Surely this was Sitting Bull, come to rescue them.

At that very moment Army scouts had also seen the dark objects far out across the plain and flashed word to the colonel's headquarters. Miles spent some very uncomfortable moments until he learned that the black dots were not mounted Sioux, but running buffalo.

Nevertheless, Sitting Bull was still a serious threat. So Miles took further steps to negotiate a surrender. He had the truce flag run up again, set Joseph on his feet, and exchanged him for the lieutenant. What he said or did when he learned that the young man had been well treated is not known.

When Joseph rejoined his people, Looking Glass and White Bird questioned him over and over, trying to trap him into saying that he had agreed to a surrender. Joseph replied steadfastly that he had not. Looking Glass was not convinced, even after artillery fire once more exploded along the creek bottom.

All the Indians suffered another night of freezing temperature, dampness and hunger. But to these discomforts was added outright terror. The people knew that Cut-Arm and his men had joined up with their attackers. Surely tomorrow the people would be shot down like dogs.

Over in the Army camp, the colonel was not overjoyed to learn that General Howard was in sight. Now his hopes for glory were wiped out. Still, he summoned his staff and rode out to meet his commanding officer.

Witnesses claimed that the two exchanged salutes, dismounted, and shook hands. The general is supposed to have said: "Hello, Miles! I'm glad to see you. I thought you might have met Gibbon's fate. Why didn't you let me know?"

The colonel supposedly replied in frigid tones that he had despatched several messengers to apprise the general of his whereabouts, that he had succeeded in trapping the enemy, and that he was about to conclude negotiations for a surrender. It wasn't his fault that the messages had not been delivered to the general.

While the general was relieved to hear that the Nez Percés had been run to the ground, he sensed the reason underlying Miles's frosty behavior. Since the scramble for promotions and glory had been an inseparable part of his own career, he was not surprised at the cool reception given him. In spite of the weariness and frustration of the pursuit that had brought the Nez Percés to the point where this younger, more vigorous, and less exhausted officer could effect the final capture, he said kindly: "I have not come to rob you of any credit, Colonel. I know you are after a star, and I shall stand back and let you receive the surrender."

Immediately Miles's attitude changed. He became cordial and thanked General Howard "for all he had said."

The next morning was Friday, October 5, and bitterly cold. The two military leaders talked lengthily about how best to secure a surrender. Again the records that have come down to us disagree on several points. Apparently Miles told the general that he had promised the Nez Percés that if they would surrender, he would take them to the Tongue River for the winter and then return them to their own country in the spring. General Howard could accept this because his instructions were to treat the Indians "as prisoners of war in your own Department." This meant returning them to their reservation in Idaho.

Joseph was to claim later that the officers promised to return his people to the Wallowa. He was mistaken, though it might have been due to faulty interpreting.

At the conclusion of their conference, General Howard summoned Ad Chapman. He told him to take Captain John and Old George, two Treaty Nez Percés who had accompanied him on the entire seventeen hundred mile journey, to the Nez Percé camp and discuss the terms of surrender. The terms were fair because Howard promised that if the Indians surrendered peacefully, there would be no trials and no hangings, and that food and blankets would be given the families immediately.

Secure behind the white truce flag which they knew Joseph would honor, the delegation rode toward the creek. When some of the warriors peered out, Captain John called, "All my brothers, I am glad to see you alive this sun! We have traveled a long ways trying to catch you. We are glad to hear you want no more war, do not want to fight."

The warriors were enraged. No one dared say they did not want to fight, especially two traitors! They leaped up to kill them. But Joseph stopped them. While his warriors spat on Captain John and called him *Jokais,* which meant *worthless,* Joseph made it clear he would not talk until the two went away. When they scuttled off, he and Chapman sat down to talk. They palavered so long that Miles sent a messenger over to remind Joseph that he wished to end the war that day.

By this time Looking Glass and White Bird had joined

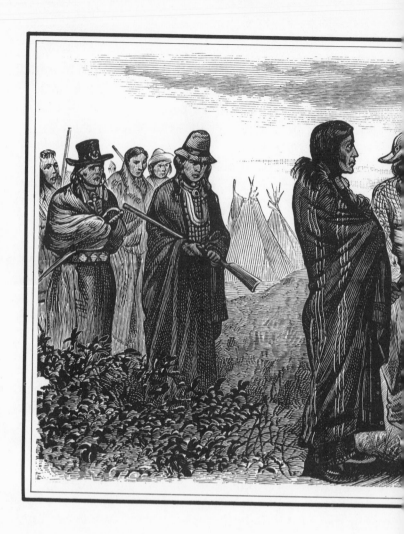

Colonel Nelson A. Miles
accepts the surrender of Chief
Joseph. From a sketch made
at the scene by G. M. Holland.

the talk. They heard Miles's message. Joseph said quickly, "You see, it is true enough. I did not say, 'Let's quit!'"

Looking Glass nodded. "Yes, we believe you now."

Chapman withdrew then because Joseph said the chiefs must talk among themselves. He promised to report to the truce robe later.

Looking Glass warned Joseph, "If you surrender, you will be sorry." He reminded him what had happened to other chiefs who listened to "a man with two faces and two tongues."

Joseph could not be dissuaded from surrendering. He said what the others knew to be true, that the women and children were freezing and starving. "For myself, I do not care. It is for them I am going to surrender."

White Bird bristled. He would never surrender! Looking Glass declared, "I will never surrender to a deceitful white chief." After more talk these two agreed that during the night they and their people would steal away and run for the camp of Sitting Bull. Joseph accepted this because it was the Nez Percé way to allow a man to act on his own.

At that instant, one of the warriors secreted among the rocks shouted that a man on horseback was racing toward them from the north. Thinking this surely was a messenger from Sitting Bull, Looking Glass leaped to his feet to see for himself. The second his face appeared in the sights of a soldier's rifle, he was shot in the head and died instantly. The warriors were so stunned that none leaped to help their fallen leader. This was the final betrayal.

So it was the women who rushed in and took up the mourning. It is said that Joseph and White Bird stumbled back to their shelters and sat alone on the ground, engulfed in abject misery. After a while, Joseph rose and called for a pony. When one was brought to him, he mounted and laid his rifle across the pommel of the saddle. Because his shirt and leggings were frayed from bullet holes, one of the women offered him a blanket. After he put it over his shoulders, he nudged the pony and rode slowly toward the white flag and parley robe.

General Howard, Colonel Miles, and several others walked out to meet him. Joseph dismounted, stepped to the general, and offered him the rifle. The General motioned that it was to be given to Colonel Miles. When the colonel accepted it, Joseph began to speak slowly, a phrase at a time. Ad Chapman translated for the officers, and a young lieutenant named Wood wrote down every word.

After saying that the chiefs were killed and the children freezing, Joseph concluded, "Hear me, my chiefs, I am tired. My heart is sick and sad. From where the sun now stands, I will fight no more forever."

The words brought such lumps to the white men's throats that none could speak. When Joseph pulled his blanket over his head, the bitter retreat to the Bear Paw came to an end.

XVI   The Bleak Future

The Wallowas watched the surrender from their shelters. After Joseph handed over his rifle, they emerged, a few at a time, and handed over their weapons. Most were terrified of the soldiers. But instead of killing them, the troops appeared with blankets and food. Soon fires were blazing. The young soldiers coaxed the mothers to bring their children from the freezing pits into the circles of warmth. But White Bird and many of his people, along with several families of Looking Glass's band, refused to appear. Late that night they scuttled out of camp and hastened north over the snowy plain.

One of the women described her feelings on leaving: "It was lonesome, the leaving. Husbands dead, friends buried or held prisoners. I felt that I was leaving all that

I had but I did not cry. You know how you feel when you lose kindred and friends through the sickness—death. You do not care if you die. With us it was worse. Strong men, well women, and little children killed and buried. They had not done wrong to be so killed. We had only asked to be left in our own homes, the homes of our ancestors. Our going was with heavy hearts, broken spirits. But we would be free! . . . All lost, we walked silently on into the wintry night."

About two hundred and thirty Indians left the Bear Paw battlefield that night. A few died on the journey, and some were overtaken the next day by the soldiers. Perhaps half the number met a Sioux rescue party, riding down to help the Nez Percés. When White Bird told them Joseph had surrendered, they escorted the travelers safely to Sitting Bull's camp.

How many were left on the battlefield? The military records show 87 men, 184 women and 147 children. The total figure of 418 was a little more than half of those who had set forth on the long, bitter retreat. In his official count, Colonel Miles expressed his admiration for these people, writing: "The whole Nez Percé movement is unequalled in the history of Indian warfare."

Alvin Joseph, Jr., an authority on the great retreat, provides these statistics. The Nez Percés traveled 1,700 miles, fighting much of the way with an estimated 2,000 troops and volunteer militia, in four major battles and fourteen other engagements. Their casualties included 65 men killed and 55 women and children. But, during the fighting they killed 180 white men and wounded another 150. A report issued months later put the cost of waging war against the non-Treaty Nez Percés at

$1,873,410.43, a very big sum in those days. This does not include the cost to civilians in property stolen or destroyed. Nor does it show that when the non-Treaty bands came together for their last rendezvous in Idaho, they were a strong and wealthy people. They had many horses and cattle and were rich in robes, saddles, weapons, and food. Now they were destitute and had lost their freedom.

When the long march south to Fort Keogh on the Tongue River began, Colonel Miles invited Joseph to ride at his side. The two talked lengthily. For the first time, Miles learned the Indian side of the story. He also gained enormous respect for Joseph and promised to do everything he could to help the people get back to their reservation.

But this was not to be.

General Sherman, commander-in-chief of the United States Army, announced that the Nez Percés leaders would be hanged, and the survivors shunted off to a reservation far from their homeland. In vain Colonel Miles protested. As strongly as he dared, he reminded the commander that both he and General Howard had promised there would be no executions and that the Nez Percés might go home in the spring. Naturally, he expected General Howard to support him. Thus he was dismayed to learn that General Howard supported General Sherman's decision.

Personal vanity was involved. The afternoon on which Joseph had surrendered, Colonel Miles had sent a messenger racing to Fort Keogh with the news. He took full credit for ending the war in the dispatch which was telegraphed to military headquarters and newspapers. Thus Miles, and not Howard, became the great war hero. General Howard, angered by this and smarting under the criticism heaped on his head during the long retreat, wanted to get back in the good graces of General Sherman. To justify breaking his promise to the Nez Percés, he claimed that when White Bird and his people fled to Canada, their action rendered his promise null and void.

On November 1, Colonel Miles received orders to move the Nez Percé captives from Fort Keogh, where he had seen them comfortably camped, on down the Yellowstone by flatboat to Fort Lincoln, near present-day Bismarck, North Dakota. The news frightened the Indians badly. *Ayee!* What Looking Glass and White Bird had said was true! Now they were going to be moved like cattle to a city where they all would be hanged! One of the women started a death chant that never ceased entirely, day or night, during the cold trip downriver.

But the Nez Percés were not entirely friendless. The pitiful plight of the people and the story of the promises made on the battlefield and ignored made headlines in newspapers throughout the country. Much public sympathy mounted on their behalf. Thus, when the flatboats nudged the wharf at Bismarck, a large group of citizens *welcomed* them with cheers, friendly gestures, and a peppy brass band! A delegation stepped forth to greet Joseph and invite him to a banquet in his honor. The invitation, as published in the Bismarck *Tri-Weekly Tribune* for November 21, read: "Desiring to show you our kind feelings and the admiration we have for your bravery and humanity, as exhibited in your recent conflict with the forces of the United States, we most cordially invite you to dine with us at the Sheridan House in this city."

While Joseph attended the banquet, the people were

transported to the town square. Here they were presented with gifts of warm clothing and blankets and provided with a liberal feast. Meantime, citizens bombarded the government and military officials with demands for more humane treatment for the captives. Colonel Miles appealed to General Sherman to allow Joseph and a delegation of warriors to come to the national capital and present their case. General Sherman, the Commissioner of Indian Affairs, the Secretary of War, and the Secretary of the Interior—all rejected this proposal. But one thing was gained. Public outrage over Sherman's decision to execute the Indian leaders forced the commander to "reconsider." Colonel Miles, having done all he could at that time, bade farewell to the Nez Percés.*

Under heavy guard, the dispirited and unarmed Indians were put on a train and shipped to Fort Leavenworth, Kansas. They arrived on November 27, and were shunted off to a miserable campsite. It was on the Missouri River bottomland, on damp ground between the river and a swamp. The people wallowed in filth and suffered from pneumonia, scurvy, and malaria. Much of the food dumped in their midst was not fit for human consumption.

During the following bad months, Joseph pressed hard for better treatment for his people. He was assisted by numerous white citizens who remain nameless, but whose Christian conduct did much to keep up Joseph's faith in white people. He petitioned the government for permission to return to the Idaho reservation. General Sherman disapproved it. Then Joseph asked permission to locate to a healthier campsite. General Sherman disapproved that, also.

*Shortly afterward he was promoted to the rank of general.

After more than twenty Nez Percé had died of malaria and neglect, public pressure forced Congress to appropriate money to move the Nez Percés onto the Quapaw reservation in Kansas. Next, administration for their welfare was transferred from the Army to the Bureau of Indian Affairs. General Sherman was delighted to be rid of the vexatious problem. Unfortunately, the oppressively hot, sand-and-sagebrush campsite was no better for a people raised in the mountains. Thanks to dishonest contractors, the food delivered to the people was incredibly bad. Sanitation was nonexistent. There was no medicine to treat the sick. Forty-seven more died by October. But Joseph kept up the pressure on government officials until an inspection party finally came to see if conditions were as bad as he claimed. They were. Weeks later the Nez Percés were moved to a fertile, timbered portion of the Ponca reservation. Here they fared a little better and received some seeds and cattle.

During these difficult months practically every white man who came in contact with Joseph gained admiration for him both as a man and a leader. The newspapers and magazines lauded his dignity and manliness, his courage and devotion. When he finally was given permission, in 1879, to come to Washington, D.C., throngs turned out to hear him speak. Some people expressed surprise at his appearance. They expected to see a savage, glowering figure resplendent in feathered headdress and fringed buckskin suit. Instead they looked on a tall, dignified man clad in a plain shirt and wool trousers. His dark hair was combed neatly in the pompadour and braids favored by adherents of the Dreamer faith. When he began to speak, with Ad Chapman interpreting, the audience heard

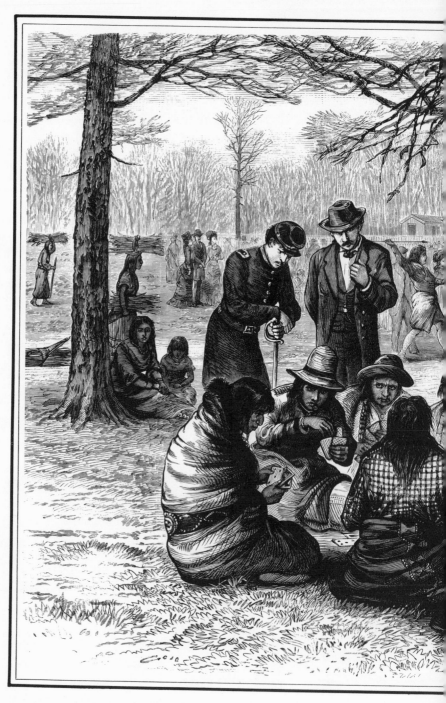

The Nez Percé prisoners amuse themselves in a temporary village on the old race course near Fort Leavenworth. From a sketch by P. J. Howell.

him say, in part: "I am tired of talk that comes to nothing. It makes my heart sick when I remember all the good words and all the broken promises. . . . If the white man wants to live in peace with the Indian, he can live in peace. There need be no trouble.

"Treat all men alike. Give them all the same law. Give them all an even chance to live and grow. . . . I know that my race must change. We cannot hold our own with the white men as we are. We only ask an even chance to live as other men live. We ask to be recognized as men. We ask that the same law shall work alike on all men. . . .

"Let me be a free man—free to travel, free to stop, free to work, free to trade where I choose, free to choose my own teachers, free to follow the religion of my fathers, free to think and talk and act for myself—and I will obey every law, or submit to the penalty."

After Joseph's speech was given nationwide distribution in newspapers, thousands of letters and petitions poured into Washington, demanding better treatment for his people. Incredibly, six years passed before the Indian Bureau decided it was "safe" to allow the Nez Percés to return to the mountains. Now only 268 were left of those who had surrendered at the Bear Paw. Of these, 118 were transferred to the reservation at Lapwai, but only after they agreed to become Christians and cut their hair. Joseph and 150 others refused to give up the Dreamer faith so they were placed on the Colville reservation in northeastern Washington. The Salish and other bands already there created so much trouble that soldiers had to be brought in to protect the Nez Percés. In time the danger passed, and the Nez Percés settled down. By 1890, thirty of the families were engaged in farming. As soon as they gathered enough skins and poles for tepees, they abandoned the comfortless shacks provided by the Indian Bureau.

Joseph steadfastly refused to believe that eastern Washington was to be his permanent home. He began pressing for permission to take his people, a mere handful of Wallowas now, back to their beloved valley. In 1900, an inspector for the Indian Bureau accompanied Joseph on a brief trip so he could visit his father's grave and see Wallowa Lake once more. He was well received by the ranchers who remembered him. But their cordiality disappeared when Joseph asked if any would sell land to the Indian Bureau so the Wallowas could return to their valley. When all refused, he still did not give up hope. Coming home to the Wallowa was an obsession now. He felt that all he need do was keep asking, keep pressing, keep fighting in his peaceful way.

Again in the summer of 1904, Joseph journeyed with government officials to the valley. Again he went from ranch to ranch, pleading for the few acres his people would need. This time the ranchers were blunt. They made it clear that they did not want Indians camping in the valley that year, the next year, a hundred years from then.

When the last door closed in his face, Joseph realized he had lost the battle to bring his people home. He was silent on the long ride back to the Colville reservation. For weeks he brooded. Then, according to the Indians, on September 21, while sitting in front of his tepee, his spirit "leaped free."

The reservation doctor said simply: "Joseph died of a broken heart."

*A photograph of Chief Joseph
taken by Delancey Gill in 1900,
after the Nez Percé had been defeated.*

Long after the Nez Percés buried the great chief in the old way with mourning and ceremony, a handsome monument was raised over his grave by the Washington State Historical Society. Several years later, well-meaning citizens began a campaign to have his remains buried at the foot of Wallowa Lake. It came to nothing. Others sought to have a suitable memorial and museum erected on the Nez Percé reservation at Lapwai. But the Idahoans had not forgotten the terrible raids of 1877. They refused to consider it.

In 1956, one of the numerous large dams being built by the government to control the Columbia River was named the Chief Joseph Dam. Erskine Wood, son of the young lieutenant who had written down Joseph's famous speech of surrender, delivered the dedicatory address. He summed up the modern historian's view of the great man, saying: "He ruled by the sheer force of his character. . . . There was no hatred in his soul in spite of the wrongs our race had done him. . . . He was a man of true magnanimity."

Today, the Nez Percés are still a divided people. Old loyalties and allegiances have carried down to the present. Of about twenty-one hundred names entered on the tribal role, some still live on the Colville reservation, some at Lapwai. Over seven hundred live in white communities. The tribal council, with government assistance, is trying to initiate programs to educate and train the people for a better life. Some respond. Many do not. They cannot. The decades of mistreatment have taken too great a toll of their spirit.

Perhaps they are waiting for another Joseph to grow to manhood among them, and lead them out of exile.

INDEX

ACKNOWLEDGEMENTS

Smithsonian Institution, National Anthropological Archives, 11, 22, 27 (lower), 71, 85, 186

New York Public Library, 14, 52–53, 80–81, 102–103

Museum of the American Indian, 27 (upper)

Culver, 30–31, 58–59, 111, 121, 133, 138–139, 144–145, 153, 156–157, 165, 168, 172–173, 182–183

Brady Handy Collection, Library of Congress, 36, 46

Royal Ontario Museum, Toronto, Canada, 64

National Portrait Gallery, Smithsonian Institution, 125

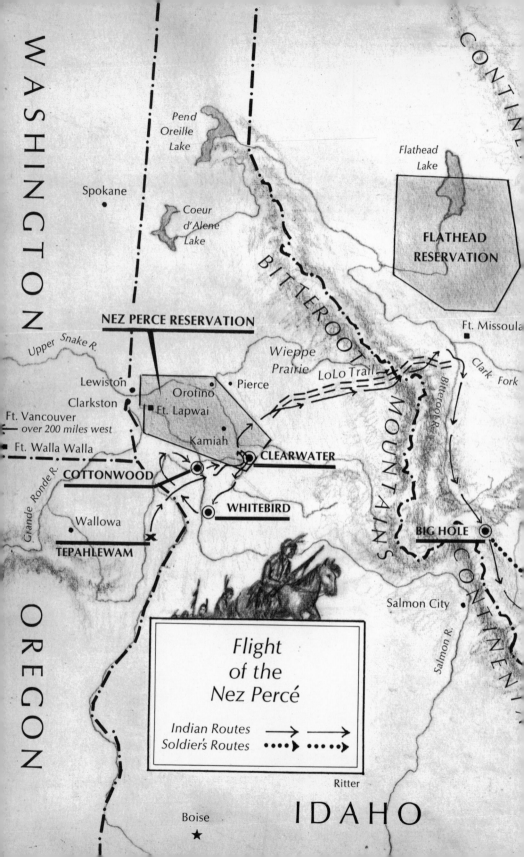

Flight
of the
Nez Percé

Indian Routes
Soldier's Routes